Cambridge Elements

Elements in the Ancient Near Eastern World and the Bible
edited by
Christopher B. Hays
*Fuller Theological Seminary and
University of Pretoria, South Africa*
Brent A. Strawn
Duke University

SEX AND SEXUALITY IN THE ANCIENT NEAR EAST

Stephanie Lynn Budin

Shaftesbury Road, Cambridge CB2 8EA, United Kingdom

One Liberty Plaza, 20th Floor, New York, NY 10006, USA

477 Williamstown Road, Port Melbourne, VIC 3207, Australia

314–321, 3rd Floor, Plot 3, Splendor Forum, Jasola District Centre,
New Delhi – 110025, India

Cambridge University Press is part of Cambridge University Press & Assessment,
a department of the University of Cambridge.

We share the University's mission to contribute to society through the pursuit of
education, learning and research at the highest international levels of excellence.

www.cambridge.org
Information on this title: www.cambridge.org/9781009559010

DOI: 10.1017/9781009559003

© Stephanie Lynn Budin 2026

This publication is in copyright. Subject to statutory exception and to the provisions
of relevant collective licensing agreements, no reproduction of any part may take
place without the written permission of Cambridge University Press & Assessment.

When citing this work, please include a reference to the DOI 10.1017/9781009559003

First published 2026

A catalogue record for this publication is available from the British Library

*A Cataloging-in-Publication data record for this Element is available from the Library
of Congress*

ISBN 978-1-009-55901-0 Hardback
ISBN 978-1-009-55902-7 Paperback
ISSN 2977-0661 (online)
ISSN 2977-0653 (print)

Cambridge University Press & Assessment has no responsibility for the persistence
or accuracy of URLs for external or third-party internet websites referred to in this
publication and does not guarantee that any content on such websites is, or will remain,
accurate or appropriate.

For EU product safety concerns, contact us at Calle de José Abascal, 56, 1°, 28003
Madrid, Spain, or email eugpsr@cambridge.org

Sex and Sexuality in the Ancient Near East

Elements in the Ancient Near Eastern World and the Bible

DOI: 10.1017/9781009559003
First published online: February 2026

Stephanie Lynn Budin
Author for correspondence: Stephanie Lynn Budin

Abstract: This Element presents what we know about the construction of sexuality and the sex lives of the residents of ancient Mesopotamia, Anatolia, and the Levant. After briefly introducing the regions and cultures under consideration and the sources of data, the Element turns to female and male experiences of sexuality, matters of fertility and infertility, sexual orientation, and finally sex crimes. Primary sources are heavily foregrounded so that readers may understand what the sources of information are on these topics and may see how scholars have come to the understandings that they have.

Keywords: sexuality, ancient Near East, Mesopotamia, biblical studies, Anatolia, Levant

© Stephanie Lynn Budin 2026

ISBNs: 9781009559010 (HB), 9781009559027 (PB), 9781009559003 (OC)
ISSNs: 2977-0661 (online), 2977-0653 (print)

Contents

What Is Sex?	1
Where and When?	1
Sources of Data	6
Types of Sex	15
Female Sexuality	19
Male Sexuality	28
Love Sickness	31
Infertility	32
Sexual Orientation	38
The Dark Side: Sexual Crimes	47
Conclusion	57
References	60

What Is Sex?

It is difficult to discuss sex in English. The problem is vocabulary. English provides one word for two distinct concepts: "sex" (the biological role an individual plays in reproduction as expressed in genes, anatomy, and gamete size) and "sex" (genital friction, generally between two or more individuals, aka intercourse, coitus). Obviously, these two concepts are related: The act of sex – sexual intercourse – between members of the opposite sexes – female and male – can lead to reproduction. Put simply, "sex" is either a biological/anatomical/physiological state or an action. This Element mainly deals with sex as the action.

In this instance, it may be better to think of the topic of this study as *eroticism*. Deriving from the name of one of the Greek deities of love and sex – Eros – eroticism is the understanding and experience of sexual desire. This can include a desire for a specific partner with whom to engage in sexual intercourse, the desire to have sexual intercourse regardless of the partner, or a desire for sexual experiences beyond the act of coitus (e.g. masturbation, romance). What we shall be considering in this Element is the gamut of erotic experiences in the ancient Near East.

Because both definitions of "sex" wind up implicating reproduction, this end result of certain forms of sexuality will play a secondary role in this work. For the most part, precisely because sex was (usually) expected to end in pregnancy, the combination of sex and reproduction shows up most commonly when fertility fails, through either the impotence/infertility of the male or the barrenness of the female. These states – impotence and barrenness – influence how people had sex, and thus this returns us to the topic of the Element.

So, this Element is a consideration of sexual desire – physical and emotional – as experienced and expressed by the inhabitants of the ancient Near East, with the notion of reproduction seen as a secondary and complicating factor rather than a primary focus.

Where and When?

What, then, is the ancient Near East (ANE)? Geographically, the ANE consists of what is now dubbed either Western Asia, the Near East, or the Middle East. It consists of Anatolia (Turkey), the Levant (Syria, Lebanon, Israel/Palestine), Cyprus, Mesopotamia (Iraq), and Elam/Persia (Iran); some people will also include Egypt and Nubia (Sudan) in that designation. See Figure 1.

Chronologically, at its greatest extent the "ancient" of ANE goes from the Paleolithic (the first archaeologically attested human occupation) through to the rise of Islam in the seventh century CE (after which point it becomes "medieval"). More typically in academia, the range is much shorter, going

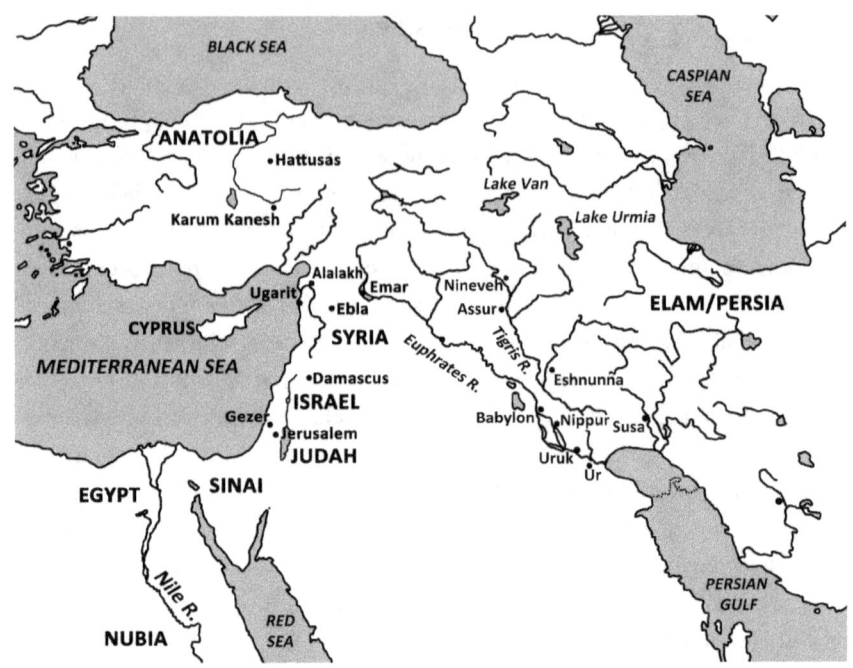

Figure 1 Map of the ancient Near East.

from the rise of writing in the late fourth millennium through to the conquests of Alexander the Great of Macedon in the late fourth century BCE (when the cultures involved go from being indigenous to a mixture of indigenous and Hellenic, later Roman). It is this more confined chronology that will appear here.

In this Element we are going to be looking at only three of the ANE geographic regions: Mesopotamia, the Levant, and to a lesser extent Anatolia (see the Ancient Egypt in Context series for more on Egypt and Nubia). All three of these have their own means of expressing chronology, and they have specific terms used to designate time, place, and culture. What follows is a very brief introduction to these chronologies and terminologies. To be clear, there are still difficulties in correlating cultural or political periods with exact dates (e.g. Akkadian Empire = 2334–2159 BCE). All the dates are technically approximate and follow what is called the Middle Chronology (the one most commonly used in academia).

Mesopotamia

2900–2334 – Early Dynastic
2334–2159 – Akkadian Empire

2159–2112 – City-state interim; Reign of Gudea of Lagaš (c. 2150–2125)
2112–2004 – Third Dynasty of Ur
2017–1792 – Isin-Larsa Period
1813–1781 – Old Assyrian Empire (Age of Samsu-Addu)
1792–1595 – Old Babylonian Empire (Age of Hammurabi)
1595–1155 – Kassite Era
1365–1031 – Middle Assyrian Empire
934–612 – Neo-Assyrian Empire
614–539 – Neo-Babylonian Empire
550–331 – Achaemenid Empire (Persia)

All the titles (e.g. Kassite Era) indicate the political organization at the time and who was primarily in control. During the Early Dynastic period individual city-states, such as Ur and Uruk, coexisted independently, ruled by a king and queen who reigned on behalf of the city's tutelary deity (Nanna for Ur, Inana for Uruk). The forces leading to the rise of greater political units – empires – had their first main success with the Akkadian Empire, when Sargon of Akkad unified all of Mesopotamia. Later such imperial conglomerations occurred under the cities of Ur (Third Dynasty of Ur), Aššur (the various Assyrian Empires), and Babylon (Babylonian Empires, including the Kassite).

Two primary language groups existed in Mesopotamia: Sumerian and Akkadian, the latter including the dialects of Babylonian and Assyrian. The former (currently) is related to no other known languages; Akkadian is a Semitic language related to Arabic and Hebrew. Both used a writing system known as cuneiform, meaning "wedge-shaped." In the earlier Sumerian the writing system was logographic, meaning that the cuneiform signs represented entire words. Thus the sign LÚ means "person" ⟨𒇽⟩ / 𒇽, while the sign MUNUS/SAL means "woman/female" ▷/𒊩 (here I show the older, more pictographic version of the sign and its later rendering in wedge-shaped cuneiform). When the Semitic Akkadian became a more popular medium, many of the logographic signs and meanings were still used but now accompanied by signs that had phonetic values. Thus the sign 𒀭, in addition to meaning "deity," could also have the reading of the sound *an*. In transliteration, Sumerian logograms appear in SMALL CAPS, phonetic readings appear in *italics*.

The Levant

3300–3050 – Early Bronze Age (EBA) I
3050–2300 – Early Bronze II–III
2300–2000 – EB IV–Middle Bronze Age (MBA) I
2000–1750 – MBA IIA

1750–1550 – MBA IIB–C (Hyksos Interlude)
1550–1400 – Late Bronze Age (LBA) I
1400–1200 – LBA II
1200–1000 – Iron Age I
1000–586 – Iron Age II
586–538 – Babylonian Captivity (Israel-Palestine)
538–330 – Persian Period

The area known as the Levant, the eastern coast of the Mediterranean Sea, can usefully be divided into three parts. To the north is Syria, which throughout much of its history was heavily influenced by Mesopotamia to the east and Anatolia to the north. On the central coast is the area that would become Iron Age Phoenicia. Although more influenced by Egypt than Mesopotamia, a defining characteristic of this area is its location on the sea and its age-old potential for sea trade and long-range colonization. Finally, there is the southern region – Israel-Palestine. In the Bronze Age it and its northern Phoenician neighbor together comprised the territory of Canaan. In the Iron Age the southern Levant consisted of the smaller states of Israel to the north, Judah to the south, and Ammon, Moab, and Edom to the east. Because so many distinct cultures and traditions are involved, the chronology often sticks with neutral terminology, for example "Late Bronze Age" with varying degrees of refinement.

The Early Bronze Age is marked by the rise of urbanism in Syria, especially the cities of Mari and Ebla. Urbanism reached a peak in the Middle Bronze Age throughout the region, with a bit of a political apogee when Canaan briefly controlled northern Egypt during the so-called Hyksos Interlude. During the Late Bronze Age the entire Levant was controlled by foreign powers – Anatolian Mitanni and then Hatti to the north (see the section "Anatolia"), Egypt to the south. After a general collapse of civilization at the break between the Bronze and Iron Ages, the Levantine city-states had a brief period of independence before again being dominated, this time by the Assyrians and Babylonians of Mesopotamia.

Syria existed within the politico-cultural domination of Anatolia and Mesopotamia. It already used Semitic languages related to Akkadian (e.g. Ugaritic) and even used forms of cuneiform for writing. Phoenicia saw in its neighboring empires potential for extensive, profitable trade; and when worse came to worst they could build really good ships and escape into the greater Mediterranean (founding colonies such as Carthage as far afield as Spain and beyond). It was mainly Israel-Palestine that had problems with foreign domination. In 722 BCE Assyria conquered Israel and dispersed its population throughout the empire. In 586 the Babylonians did the same thing to Judah. Fifty years later, once the Persians got control of Mesopotamia, the Judeans were allowed to return to their homeland, and it was in this context that the Hebrew Bible came into its earliest recognizable form.[1] Both the Phoenicians and Israelites-Judeans spoke Semitic languages which they wrote in linear alphabets.

In this Element, focus on the Levant will be on the coastal city of Ugarit for the Bronze Age and Israel-Judah in the Iron Age, owing to the availability of the sources and the extent to which these communities were similar and different regarding their Near Eastern neighbors.

Anatolia

2000–1750 – Hatti; Assyrian trading colony at Kaneš
1650–1500 – Hittite Old Kingdom
1500–1420 – Hittite Middle Kingdom
1500–1350 – Mitannian Empire
1420–c. 1200 – Hittite Empire
1200–900 – Dark Age
900–500 – Rise of the Neo-Hittite states (Urartu, Phrygia, Lydia)
c. 700 – Assyrian conquest of Urartu
Early seventh century – Conquest of Phrygia by Cimmerians and eventual domination by Lydia
545 – Persian conquest of Lydia

In the mid-second millennium BCE Anatolia came to be dominated by an Indo-European-speaking population known as the Hittites, ruled by their capital city of Hattuša (modern Boğazköy). They absorbed an earlier, indigenous population of the interior plateau known as the Hatti. From about 1500 to 1350 the Hittites lived side by side with a group called the Hurrians, speakers of a language related to Urartian who during their heyday in southeastern Anatolia and northern Mesopotamia ruled the Mitannian Empire. The Hurrians were a cultural conduit between the Hittites to the north and Mesopotamia to the east, forming a bridge between the languages and literatures of both. As a result, the religions and mythologies of Anatolia are a mixture of Hurrian and Hittite (much like the royal families), and the Hittite language is written in Mesopotamian-style cuneiform, often using logograms rather than phonetic spellings for divine names. As a result, Hittite texts will, for

---

[1] The origins of the Bible is a very long and complicated topic to say the least, and I do not even pretend to do it justice here. For a focused starting point and bibliography, the reader may wish to look at Satlow 2014.

example, refer to the goddess IŠTAR (a Mesopotamian deity) even though they are actually referring to the Hurro-Hittite goddess Šauška.

Sources of Data

Mesopotamia

Myths and Hymns

The Mesopotamians provided a wealth of material on sexuality, the most explicit of which are the mythological narratives and poetry pertaining to the goddess Inana/Ištar. One subcategory of these is the so-called *Bridal Songs*, composed in Sumerian, which revolve around the theme of the courtship of Inana and Dumuzi. While many of the texts pertaining to Inana/Ištar are probably beyond the life experience of normal, mortal females (especially the hymn where she has sex with sixty young men in the city and calls out for more), the presentation of Inana in these songs as the enthusiastic young bride and her distinctly feminine experience of sexuality (see the section "Female Sexuality") suggest that such texts may in fact give a view of sexuality in line with mortal experience. Besides, as the aphorism states, "May Inana make a hot-limbed wife lie with you!"[2] So the enjoyment of sex wasn't just for goddesses.

Many other mythological narratives present the Mesopotamian experience of eroticism, often with deities as the main players. While texts such as *Enki and the World Order* and *Gilgameš* present a particularly masculine perspective on sex, works such as *Enlil and Ninlil*, *Nergal and Ereškigal*, as well as the *Bridal Songs*, present a more feminine view.

Royal Love Songs

More secular in context, the *Royal Love Songs*, from the second millennium and composed in Sumerian, are addressed not to a deity but to the royal family, most specifically the king in his most erotic guise. Such songs may alternate in dialect between the less common EME-SAL and the more standard EME-GIR. There is ongoing debate as to the relationship between these two "dialects" or (perhaps more accurately) "sociolects," but one leading interpretation is that EME-SAL is a specifically *feminine* dialect of Sumerian, used in certain genres of literature especially when the female voice is expressed. To quote Piotr Michałowski, Sumerologist and specialist on the subject:

> [O]ne may propose that beginning perhaps as early as the late third millennium, Sumerian was, simply speaking, the poetic language. This is to say

---

[2] Proverb 1.147, https://etcsl.orinst.ox.ac.uk/cgi-bin/etcsl.cgi?text=t.6.1.01&charenc=j#.

that one must view all the ancient languages as a hierarchy within a world of discourse, and not as completely distinct entities. Within this sociolinguistic matrix Sumerian was, by its distribution, marked for poetic function pure and simple. There was even a hierarchy within Sumerian. A purely literary "dialect," designated eme-sal, literally the "high-pitched /thin language," was used only for direct speech of women and goddesses in myths and for specific ritual observances, primarily the cultic practices of the gala priests. There is much controversy about the nature of this "dialect," but for our purposes it will suffice to state that if Standard Sumerian was marked for poetic function, eme-sal was marked to an even higher degree.[3]

As such, EME-GIR (e.g. Standard Sumerian) might be understood to be ungendered/common while EME-SAL is specifically feminine in nature. If this be the case (and more research is needed), then the dialogues of the *Royal Loves Songs* might be understood as conversations between the king and female members of his household. Thus we read the words supposedly sung by Queen Kubātum to her husband after the birth of their first child:

> A gold ring and a ring of silver – the lord gave me a present!
> O lord! Your presents enhance the HI.LI (sex-appeal) so that you look at me!
> O Šu-Suen, your things enhance the HI.LI, so that you look at me![4]

Gwendolyn Leick has suggested that the *Royal Love Songs* originated in the competitive context of the polygynous royal household, where the king's wives were in competition for their lord's affections.

> Polygyny fosters sexual competition to win the favours of the "master", and expertise in erotic matters is an important factor ... Some of the love-songs, especially when they are directed at the king, could be understood as a manifestation of seduction through poetic artifice. Others, such as those which are set in the form of a dialogue between lovers, are a stylistic variation of the same scenario ... We know that royal wives "composed", or at least commissioned, literary compositions ... I would like to believe that they represent the "true" voice of Sumerian women.[5]

Magico-Medical Texts

The Mesopotamians had an extensive corpus of texts pertaining to health and healing. These include anatomical lexica, medical diagnostic and prognosis documents, identification of demons who could afflict the human body, and

---

[3] Michałowski 1996: 147. For more on this subject, see Whittaker 2002.   [4] Leick 1994: 114.
[5] Leick 1994: 112–113.

both medical and magical (different to us, not them) cures for these various and sundry ailments and afflictions. Entries in the lists of ailments begin with a *šumma* – "If" – clause, list the symptoms, and provide the diagnosis at the end. Thus:

> If the top of his head continually feels as if split in two all day/night long, he continually has sexual desires, and the bedding is continually turned around him, (and) like one who lays himself down on top of a woman he has an erection, [it is] the "hand" of Ardat Lilî [a demon].[6]

Some texts dealt more extensively with sexual matters than others. Notable in this regard are the ŠÀ.ZI.GA (Akkadian *nīš libbi*), or "rising of the 'heart'" texts, which deal with erectile dysfunction.[7] They date to the Old Babylonian period (a small fragment exists from this time),[8] although most preserved texts date to the Middle Babylonian period and have come to light in both Mesopotamia and the Hittite capital at Boğazköy.[9]

More in the realms of magic than medicine were the love (*râmu*) and hate (*zêru*) spells, dating as far back as the Akkadian Empire period.[10] The former attracted a beloved; the latter broke up a couple, or dissuaded possible liaisons. As noted by F. A. M. Wiggermann, some of the regular activities of the *āšipu* (magic-user) pertained to "love of a man for a woman," "love of a woman for a man," and "love of a man for a man."[11] Both sexes could take the initiative in love magic.

Omen Texts

The Mesopotamians took a deep interest in divination, the king especially, and thus numerous omen texts pertaining to all aspects of reality have come down to us from antiquity. Like the medical texts, entries in the omen texts begin with *šumma* clauses, describe the scenario in question, and then offer the resultant prognosis. Thus, "If a man ejaculates in his dream and is spattered with his semen, that man will find riches; he will have financial gain."[12]

The sex omens are a subset of the first-millennium *Šumma Ālu* series – "If a city ... " – appearing on tablets 103 and 104. Tablet 103 has thirty-two omens pertaining to sexual acts with women (the subject of the omens is always assumed to be male), including different sexual positions. Tablet 104 contains thirty-eight omens and documents a broader spectrum of sexual behaviors, including homoerotic acts and masturbation.[13]

---

[6] Scurlock 2014: 102. [7] Biggs 2002, 1967; Zisa 2021. [8] Zisa 2021: 3.
[9] Zisa 2021: 4. [10] Zsolnay 2014: 280. [11] Wiggermann 2010: 414. See also Zisa 2021: 178.
[12] Guinan 1997: 466. [13] Guinan 2022: 186.

Legal Texts

The law codes provide data on the social construct of sexual norms. In them we see how the Mesopotamians viewed matters such as adultery and rape, as well as issues of marriage, divorce, barrenness, and infertility. Legal texts such as marriage contracts and last wills also provide data on interpersonal relationships, including the sexual.

Anatolia

Myths

The Hurrians and Hittites left behind a smaller corpus of mythological material than did their Mesopotamian neighbors. Even so, there are several texts that feature aspects of sexuality that provide data on the Hittite and Hurrian view of eroticism, notably the *Song of Ullikummi* (wherein the goddess Šauška tried to seduce the monster Ullikummi), the *Song of Ḫedammu* (where the goddess Šauška does seduce the monster Ḫedammu), the *Tale of Illuyanka* (where the goddess Inara has sex with the hero to get him to defeat the story's villain), and the *Song of Kumarbi* (where the god Kumarbi gets pregnant).

Law Code

The text known as the *Hittite Laws* (HL) is a Hittite corpus of approximately 200 legal clauses. While the oldest preserved version dates back to the Old Kingdom, c. 1650 BCE, references in the text to earlier versions suggest that at least some of the laws may actually be much earlier. The *Hittite Laws* were maintained and slightly updated throughout Hittite history, with a notable softening of penalties over the course of time (e.g. crimes that used to be punishable by death later resort merely to banishment). Generally speaking, the law code is not a particularly well-organized affair. To quote Trevor Bryce:

> The collection presents a largely unsystematic jumble of civil and criminal law. It has all the signs of being a hodge-podge of a number of separate contributions, perhaps accumulated over a period of many years. And from the hundreds, perhaps thousands, of court judgements on which it might have drawn there appears to have been a considerable element of randomness in what actually went into it.[14]

In spite of this random, hodge-podge nature the laws pertaining to sexuality are well organized, consisting of §§187–200. Most involve forbidden sexual liaisons, including bestiality, rape, and adultery. As was common throughout

---

[14] Bryce 2002: 35.

the ANE, incest was seen as especially problematic, while homosexuality was not even addressed.

Magico-Medical Texts

As noted in the section on Mesopotamian magico-medical texts, a copy of the ŠÀ.ZI.GA text was discovered at Boğazköy (ancient Hattuša), and thus we may suppose that the Hittites were just as concerned about erectile dysfunction as their neighbors. A distinctly Hittite text that also deals with the matter of male sexual dysfunction is *Paškuwatti's Ritual*, composed in the Middle Hittite period but known from a single tablet dating to the thirteenth century BCE.[15] As we shall see in the section on infertility, the exact nature of the male patient's dysfunction remains in debate. The usual suggestion is that the man suffers from some kind of erectile dysfunction. However, a more recent argument made by Jared Miller suggests that the patient must be cured of homosexuality, at least enough that he might have successful intercourse with his wife.[16]

Curses

When making treaties in the ANE curses were employed at the end to make sure all sides kept their words. While death, devastation, and destruction were common in these formulae, every so often they would also include references to sexuality. Thus a treaty from Anatolia threatens to deprive the enemies' women of love and sexuality, just as an Assyrian peace treaty between King Aššur-nerari V of Assyria and King Mati'-ilu of Arpad threatens, "May Mati'-ilu's (sex) life be that of a mule, his wives extremely old!" should that king betray his trust.[17]

The Levant

Ugarit

The material from Ugarit is primarily literary-mythological. While the site revealed numerous texts pertaining to ritual, archives, and foreign relations, only the myths and legends give any insight into sexuality. Such works include the *Ba'al Cycle* (where the god Ba'al has sex with a cow seventy times in a row), *The Tale of Aqhat*, the *Tale of Kirta*, and the *Birth of the Gracious Gods* (where the elderly deity El has sex with a pair of young women).

---

[15] Hoffner 1987: 280.   [16] Miller 2010.
[17] Text and translation from Parpola and Watanabe 1988, accessed via http://oracc.museum.upenn.edu/saao/saa02/corpus.

Complementing the literary texts are legal texts, especially last wills and marriage contracts. Unlike the mythological texts which are written in Ugaritic, a Semitic language written in an alphabetic form of cuneiform, the legal texts are usually written in Akkadian and show influences from both Mesopotamia and Anatolia.

Israel-Judah

Our main source here is the Hebrew Bible. This is not an ideal situation. Granted, the Bible is technically a compilation of some of the sources of data presented in the other regions: myth, literature, law. But the myth is predicated on the existence of a single male deity who is minimally physical and not at all sexual. Thus the Bible is bereft of one of the primary sources present in the other regions: tales of divine sexuality. The biblical literary texts (e.g. the Psalms) are not erotic, leaving the sole poem the *Song of Songs* as a source for romance and eroticism. Only the laws, especially those of Leviticus and Deuteronomy, provide equivalent data to what we see in Mesopotamia and Anatolia.

Basically, the Bible does not present an *experience* of sexuality. And I would argue that, with the possible exception of the *Song of Songs*, this is because the Bible never presents a female voice or a female perspective on anything, and certainly not on sex or eroticism. As we shall see, the experience of sexuality was gendered in the ANE. While both sexes certainly enjoyed sex, notions of fertility were gendered masculine, as males were seen as the founts of fertility (semen).[18] By contrast, the feminine expression of sexuality focused far more on the physical pleasure of sex, especially when expressed by goddesses such as Ištar. In fact, and perhaps understandably, the feminine enjoyment of sex was enhanced by a *lack* of focus on fertility and reproduction.[19]

Furthermore, the beauty that leads to seduction and sex is a feminine attribute – it is a source of female power in the ANE literatures.[20] The Bible does not often highlight female power. As such, the narratives that the Bible does share with its ANE neighbors tend to get reimagined to deprive women of sexual power and agency. For example: A common motif in ANE literature is a scene where a female (goddess or woman) seduces a man by taking a bath in front of him (getting wet and naked).[21] Thus in Mesopotamia we have in the story of *Nergal and Ereškigal* a scene where:

> She [Ereškigal] went to the bath
> And dressed herself in a fine dress

---

[18] Budin 2023: 144–150; Budin 2019; Budin 2015.   [19] Budin 2023: 67–71.
[20] Budin 2023: 54–60.   [21] Budin 2023: 60–67.

> And allowed him [Nergal] to catch a glimpse of her body
> He [gave in to] his heart's [desire to do what men and women do].
> The two embraced each other
> And went passionately to bed.[22]

They wind up married. Such narratives appear in the literatures from Mesopotamia, Anatolia, and even Egypt. But when this same motif appears in the Bible, it is inverted, becoming not a scene of seduction but a tale of rape (2 Samuel 11:2):

> One evening David got up from his bed and walked around on the roof of the palace. From the roof he saw a woman bathing. The woman was very beautiful, and David sent someone to find out about her. The man said, "She is Bathsheba, the daughter of Eliam and the wife of Uriah the Hittite." Then David sent messengers to get her. She came to him, and he slept with her.

So we are limited in the kinds of data we can derive from the Bible. We get legal ideals and male perspectives (thus lots of reproduction and the infamous "Begats"), but many aspects of sexuality – pleasure, seduction, romance – are left out or appropriated for other narrative ends.

Finally, we must recall that the Bible is actually many books in one. Written by many authors over the course of centuries before being edited and collated and edited again with who knows how many additions, redactions, and typos thrown in, no individual passage in the Bible can necessarily reflect the same worldview or culture as any other passage. The laws presented in Leviticus – specifically the Holiness Code – need not agree with laws in Deuteronomy, and neither of those necessarily pertain to the relationships we see in Genesis, which is why, as we shall see, it can be simultaneously forbidden (Leviticus 18:16, 20:21) and mandatory (Genesis 38) to have sex with your dead brother's widow.

To sum up thus far: In general, we might divide the ANE sources into two broad categories: fiction and nonfiction. The myths and literature and poetry (and, really, the omen texts) are *fiction*. They are useful because they provide an idea of how people *thought* about things. But we cannot mistake them for reality. Inana is to sex what Batman is to crime-fighting: a fantasy and an ideal, but not actual mundane reality. *Nonfiction* is made up of the laws (to the extent they were followed, at any rate) and legal contracts, and to a certain extent the magico-medical texts. Whether or not one believes in magic, the cures themselves were implemented and influenced the sex lives of those who used them.

---

[22] Dalley 1989: 171.

Figure 2 Old Babylonian plaque with erotic scene. Vorderasiatisches Museum, Berlin VA 14514. Drawing by Paul C. Butler.

The Problem with Art

The ANE has provided a wealth of images that might be considered erotic: Old Babylonian plaques with images of couples in bed or having sex *a tergo*, Assyrian lead plaques with couples having sex on walls, and Levantine images of nude women holding their breasts have been used to argue for the presence of fertility cults, orgies, and (sacred) prostitution for decades (Figures 2–6).

But things are seldom straightforward. One must consider that these images had symbolic meanings and practical-magical uses that influenced their iconography more so than any attempts at necessarily portraying reality. For example, in her analysis of the *coitus a tergo* scenes (Figure 3), Julia Assante argues that both aspects of the sex-*cum*-drinking iconography appeal to the goddess Inana/Ištar, who claims in one of her hymns of self-praise to be a "loving ḫarimtu in the tavern" (more on this in the section on the KAR.KID/*Ḫarīmtu*). The combination of joyful sexuality and beer consumption draws the goddess's gaze and goodwill, serving as a source of blessing for the context in which such a plaque

Figure 3 Old Babylonian plaque with scene of sex *a tergo*. Vorderasiatisches Museum, Berlin VA 6214. Drawing by Paul C. Butler.

was displayed.[23] By contrast, concerning the Assyrian lead plaques (Figure 4) Assante notes that "The truth is, such lead reliefs show foreign captives performing bizarre sexual acts for Assyrian viewers and thus carry strong political messages that equate sex and visual possession with territorial conquest."[24]

When a terracotta female holds her breasts, we assume either eroticism and/or fertility/lactation imagery (Figure 5). The Judean pillar figurines from eighth-to-sixth-century Judah (Figure 6) are often taken to be the maternal goddess Asherah, who is also associated with pillars in the Bible. These figurines are described as "holding" their "pendulous" breasts, thus symbols of milky fertility. But the vast majority actually do not "hold" their breasts – their hands rest upon the abdomen in a posture of "polite attention"[25] that dates back to the third millennium in the ANE. Furthermore, when painting is discernable upon these figurines, they highlight the eyes, *not* the breasts.[26] All in all, such images – who look directly at the viewer in a pose of attentiveness – are far more likely to be conduits of prayer between mortals and deities than any goddess. One might liken them to Byzantine icons, or

---

[23] Assante 2002: 30–36.   [24] Assante 2003: 15.   [25] Suter 2000: 261–262.
[26] Ben Shlomo and McCormick 2021: 30. See also McCormick 2023.

Figure 4 Middle Assyrian lead relief of man and woman having sex on a wall. From Aššur. Vorderasiatisches Museum, Berlin VA 4244. Drawing by Paul C. Butler.

modern depictions of the Virgin Mary who looks upon the one who prays and transmits prayers to a more remote, and intimidating, God the Father.

Types of Sex[27]

Genital

The mere fact that the residents of the ANE managed to reproduce successfully is clear evidence that they engaged in heterosexual genital intercourse. Frequent reference in the love songs to females either divine (Inana) or mortal reveling in their vulvae show the importance of the female genitals in women's sexual pleasure, just as the myths make it quite clear that, when it came to sex for males, it was all about the penis. A common motif in the poetry is that such-and-such a woman's vulva is "sweet like beer,"[28] while in the sex omens the text

---

[27] The vast majority of the data in this section comes from Mesopotamia, which has provided more and more varied sources than all the other regions combined on this particular topic.

[28] Mesopotamian beer was made from dates and contained no bittering agents like hops. So their beer was, in fact, sweet.

Figure 5 Terracotta Qudšu plaque from Gezer. Ashmolean Museum 1912.621. Drawing by Paul C. Butler.

claims, "If a man repeatedly stares at his woman's vagina, his health will be good; he will lay his hands on whatever is not his."[29]

Nevertheless, there appears to have been a general disapproval (on the part of males, our main authors?) of female superior sex. The same corpus of omens claims that, "If a man, a woman mounts him, that woman will take his vigor; for one month he will not have a personal god."[30] Other positions referred to in the Mesopotamian omen texts have the female standing, bent over (much as with the abovementioned terracotta plaques), lying on her back, seated upon a chair, or even in a doorway, on a boat, or in an animal pen.[31] The residents of the ANE were hardly "missionary-only."

Cunnilingus

The idea that a woman's vulva could be "sweet like beer" may serve as a reference to cunnilingus. One of the most explicit such references appears in

---

[29] Guinan 1997: 473. [30] Guinan 1997: 473. [31] Guinan 2002: 187–188.

Sex and Sexuality in the Ancient Near East

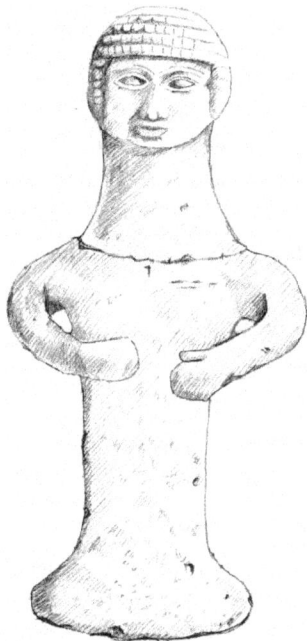

Figure 6 Judean pillar figurine from Tel Duweir. Metropolitan Museum of Art, gift of H. P and D. Colt, 1934. Drawing by Paul C. Butler.

the *Royal Love Song* to Šu-Suen. Here of the tapstress Il-ummiya the text proclaims:

> The beer of my ... Il-ummiya, the "tapstress" is sweet!
> And her vulva is sweet like beer – and her beer is sweet!
> And her vulva is sweet like her mouth and her beer is sweet!
> Her *kašbir*-beer and her (regular) beer are sweet.[32]

Another possible reference ("making tongue" in sex) indicates that such sexual technique could/did lead to orgasm:

> The "brother"[33] brought me into his house,
> He lay me down on the honey-fragrant bed,
> And when my dear sweet-heart had lain very close to me,
> One-by-one, making tongue, one-by-one,
> My fair faced "brother" did fifty.
> As if dumb struck, I moved toward him,
> Trembling below, I pushed quietly to him.
> My "brother," hand placed on his thigh,
> My dear sweet-heart, so did I pass the time there.[34]

---

[32] Assante 2002: 34; Leick 1994: 114.   [33] A term of endearment, not incest.
[34] Cooper 1997: 94. Tablet UM 29–16-8.

Anal

There are few references to heterosexual anal intercourse in the ANE documents, although in the Mesopotamian texts it is presented as being less fulfilling than genital intercourse. For example, in the abovementioned love poem to Šu-Suen, reference is made to Il-ummiya's *kašbir*-beer, generally recognized as inferior to "regular" beer. This line comes after a list referring to Il-ummiya's other orifices – vagina, mouth – and Julia Assante has argued that the reference to *kašbir*-beer is a reference to her final sexual orifice – the anus.[35] In this we may have reference to Il-ummiya's *bāb šuburri* – the "anal door" as opposed to her *bāb ūri*, the "genital door."

The inferior quality of anal sex to vaginal sex appears in the Akkadian magico-medical texts, where one finds a curse that the desired man's penis "strike (the rival) woman so-and-so in the anus, so that he cannot satisfy himself with her":

> I am the daughter of Ningirsu, the releaser. My mother is a releaser; my father is a releaser. I who have come, I really can release. May the penis of [m]PN be a stick of *martû*-wood. May it "kill" the anus of [f]PN; may he never be sated with her charms.[36]

An unusually practical omen text claims: "If a man 'goes' to the rectum of a woman ... from out of the rectum he 'goes' to the vagina – (demon) Saghullhazu will enter her; either the male or the female will die."[37]

Legal and omen texts from Mesopotamia refer to male–male anal intercourse. Most explicit is omen CT 39 44:13 from the seventh-century BCE omen compilation *Šumma ālu*, which states, "If a man (NA=*awīlum*) penetrates (TE=*sahālu*)) his social peer via the buttocks/anus (*ana* GU.DU), that man will become foremost among his brothers and colleagues."[38] From the Middle Assyrian Law Code (MAL) comes §20: "If a man has sex with his peer (and) they prove the charges against him and find him guilty, they will have sex with him and turn him into/over to a *ša rēši*."[39] Anal intercourse is likely.[40]

In the Hebrew Bible the closest we come to a reference to homosexual anal intercourse appears in passages Leviticus 18:22 and 20:13, with references to a man lying with another man "as with a woman." The language isn't exactly explicit, but anal intercourse seems to be at issue.

---

[35] Assante 2002: 34.
[36] Scurlock 2014: 108; see also Biggs 2002: 72. [m]PM refers to a male personal name, while [f]PN refers to a female personal name.
[37] Guinan 2002: 188.   [38] Guinan 1997: 469.   [39] Guinan and Morris 2017: 169.
[40] More on both of these passages in the section on "Homosexuality."

Fellatio

A possible (but uncertain) reference to fellatio appears in the Sumerian tale of *Inana and Enki*. Here, the god, drunk, gives away the core elements of civilization – the ME – to Inana. Along with various priesthoods and musical instruments, sexual intercourse and ĝeš₃.kı?.su.ub = "kissing the penis" are mentioned.[41] This, plus possible allusions to fellatio in the terracotta *coitus a tergo* drinking scenes mentioned in the previous section, is the sole evidence for female reciprocation of the abovementioned cunnilingus.

It should be noted that there are several references in the ANE mythology to male deities who swallow semen and become pregnant. In the Anatolian *Song of Kumarbi* the eponymous god bites off the genitals of his rival, the sky god Anu, and winds up pregnant with four deities. In the Egyptian New Kingdom narrative of *Horus and Seth* the goddess Isis (Horus's mother) tricks Seth into eating Horus's semen by placing it into Seth's favorite vegetable (lettuce); Seth ends up pregnant with the solar disk. And in the Mesopotamian myth *Enki and Ninhursag*, after Enki has had sex with – and impregnated – his daughter, granddaughter, and great-granddaughter, Ninhursag tricks him into eating his own semen and he becomes pregnant with several plant deities, not one of whom he can give birth to. When the ingestion of semen occurs in the ANE literature, it tends to involve castration, female trickery, extreme discomfort, and just desserts.

Female Sexuality

Females in the ANE were literally considered to be the "fairer" sex: Beauty was an aspect of feminine gender, and this beauty was understood to be erotic in nature. Rather than being responsible for fertility as men were, females – both mortal and divine – inspired sexual arousal and enjoyed the consequences thereof. Some texts even refer to sex as "that which pertains to women." Thus a Sumerian hymn to the sun god Utu records what is apparently a very young Inana telling her brother (ll. 137–140):

> I am one who knows not that which is womanly – men
> I am one who knows not *that which is womanly – copulating*
> I am one who knows not *that which is womanly – kissing*
> I am one who knows not copulating, I am one who knows not kissing.[42]

---

[41] Glassner 1992: 63.   [42] Kramer 1985: 127. Tablet BM 23631.

On tablet 1 of the Standard version of the *Gilgameš Epic*, the huntsman trying to thwart the wild man Enkidu sends the *ḫarīmtu* Šamhat to seduce him, telling her (ll. 180–185):

> There he is Šamhat! Bare your breasts,
> Spread your legs, let him take in your charms.
> Do not recoil but take in his scent;
> He will see and approach you.
> Spread your clothing so he may lie on you;
> *Do for the man the work of a woman!*[43]

Likewise, a curse from Anatolia reveals how the eroticism of women (along with motherhood) is as innately a part of femininity as fertility and warfare are of masculinity. Thus, "The Ritual and Prayer to Ištar of Nineveh" (CTH 716.1, ll. 51–58), (excerpted):

> Then from the men take away masculinity, fertility, and health; take away weapons – bows, arrows, and daggers – and bring them to Hatti Land ...
> From the women take away motherhood, love, and sexuality and bring them to Hatti Land.[44]

Female Enjoyment

While in modern times there is a somewhat Victorian notion that women are supposed to be less interested in sex than men, in the ANE it was absolutely the case that women were supposed to enjoy their sexuality. For no character was this more so than the Mesopotamian goddess of love and war Inana-Ištar. In a *pāru* hymn to the goddess we read:

> The young men of your city gather to me. Celebration is the foundation to the city!
> To the shade of the city wall let us go. Celebration is the foundation to the city!
> Seven (at) her bosom, seven (at) her hips. Celebration is the foundation to the city!
> Sixty and sixty climax in her vulva. Celebration is the foundation to the city!
> The young men got tired, Ištar did *not* tire. Celebration is the foundation to the city![45]

In perhaps a more demure moment she converses with her bridegroom Dumuzi in a *Bridal Song*:

> "This vulva, ..., like a horn, ... a great wagon, this moored Boat of Heaven ... of mine, clothed in beauty like the new crescent moon, this waste land abandoned in the desert ... this field of ducks where my ducks sit, this high well-watered field of mine: my own vulva, the maiden's, a well-watered opened-up mound – who will be its ploughman? My

---

[43] George 1999: 7, adapted.   [44] Wegner 1981: 59, my translation from the German.
[45] Von Soden and Oelsner 1991: 341, rev. ll. 14–19.

vulva, the lady's, the moist and well-watered ground – who will put an ox there?"

"Lady, the king shall plough it for you; Dumuzi the king shall plough it for you."

"Plough my vulva, man of my heart!"[46]

As Gwendolyn Leick noted of this passage:

> It is hardly a coincidence that the description of the vulva in the text above captures the stages of sexual excitement in the woman. At the beginning her vulva resembles the narrow curve of the new moon until it opens "like a boat with its mooring ropes" (more likely to refer to the labia minora than pubic hair). Then there are several references to the transudation of the mucous membranes ("well-watered low land", "my vulva, a wet place") at which point she cries out for the "plough".[47]

One question raised by such poetry is the extent to which the experience of sexuality here expressed applied to normal women rather than goddesses. The ritual contexts in which such poetry was used/recited strongly suggests male authorship, perhaps removing the sentiments expressed from the direct realms of the feminine.

Nevertheless, Jerrold Cooper has argued that in spite of the sacred and public context of this corpus, the emotions expressed may well derive from a women's tradition and so present a female voice. As he has noted, "We have no information about Sumerian women's secular songs or poetry, nor would we expect to, given the nature of our sources ... [But] [t]he odds are very good that if the Sumerian love songs are in a women's voice, there could have been an actual genre of women's love and wedding songs that served as their model."[48] That is to say, the songs hymned to Inana and Dumuzi may derive from a women's oral tradition of erotic poetry, here deemed especially important because of the sex of the goddess so honored.[49]

Furthermore, the romantic sentiments expressed in the love songs contrast with the more aggressive and fertility-oriented themes in the more masculine erotic poetry from Mesopotamia. Tales such as *Enki and the World Order*, *Enki and Ninhursag*, and *Enlil and Ninlil* present male deities reveling in their own phallic prowess, orgasms, and the resultant life, be it aquatic, vegetal, or offspring.[50] By contrast, the love songs present the female experience of sexuality as sensual, fully corporal (as opposed to merely genital), and utterly devoid of the resultant fertility (= pregnancy) so significant in the male expression of sexuality.[51] For these reasons, it is likely that the Sumerian love songs do indeed present a feminine experience of sexuality.

---

[46] A *balbale* to Inana (Dumuzid-Inana P). ETCSL translation: t.4.08.16.
[47] Leick 1994: 91–92.   [48] Cooper 1997: 89, excerpted.   [49] Wiggermann 2010: 412.
[50] Budin 2015, 2019.   [51] Cooper 1997: 95.

Furthermore, erotic bliss was not reserved exclusively for deities. Love songs with no reference to divinity also attest to the feminine enjoyment of sex. Thus in a love song to her husband King Šu-Suen the Queen declares:

> O! my lord and good spirit, my lord and guardian angel,
> My Šu-Suen, who does Enlil's heart good,
> The place where, could you but do your sweet thing to me,
> Where, could you but – like honey – put in your sweetness!
> O squeeze it in there for me, as flour into the measuring cup!
> O pound and pound it in there for me, as flour into the old, dry measuring cup![52]

Perhaps one of the most influential ANE love songs in the Western tradition is the biblical *Song of Songs*. Even here there is evidence that mortal women could take part in the joys of passionate romance. In the midst of masculine verses extolling the beauty of the "bride" (7:1–4):

> How beautiful your sandaled feet,
>   O prince's daughter!
> Your graceful legs are like jewels,
>   the work of an artist's hands.
> Your navel is a rounded goblet
>   that never lacks blended wine.
> Your waist is a mound of wheat
>   encircled by lilies.
> Your breasts are like two fawns,
>   like twin fawns of a gazelle.
> Your neck is like an ivory tower.

We also hear of the girl's love of her "bridegroom" and her desire for sex (e.g. 5:2–6):

> I slept but my heart was awake.
>   Listen! My beloved is knocking:
> "Open to me, my sister, my darling,
>   my dove, my flawless one.
> My head is drenched with dew,
>   my hair with the dampness of the night."
> I have taken off my robe –
>   must I put it on again?
> I have washed my feet –
>   must I soil them again?
> My beloved thrust his hand through the latch-opening;
>   my heart began to pound for him.
> I arose to open for my beloved,
>   and my hands dripped with myrrh,

---

[52] Jacobsen 1987: 88–89. Slightly adapted.

> my fingers with flowing myrrh,
> on the handles of the bolt.
> I opened for my beloved . . .

Sexual pleasure – as well as maternity – was deemed so important for females in Mesopotamia that those denied these pleasures turned into Lilītu or Ardat-Lilî demons after death, malevolent ghosts who broke into homes to terrorize young women and men. The description given in the medical corpus defines the Ardat-Lilî such:

> Ardat-Lilî slips in a man's window; young girl not fated (to be married); young woman who was never impregnated like a woman; young woman who was never deflowered like a woman; young girl who never experienced sexual pleasure in her husband's lap; young girl who never removed a garment in her husband's lap; young woman whose garment-pin a good man never loosened; young woman in whose breasts there never was milk, who cries in pain; young girl who was never filled with sexual pleasure in the lap of a young man, who never had her fill of desire.[53]

The "hand" of Ardat-Lilî sickened her victims, often in a sexual fashion, such as the young man we met earlier with headaches and priapism. Sexual pleasure was very important for ANE women.

Seduction

Because goddesses and women were supposed to enjoy sex, in the literature at least they often took the initiative in sexual encounters. One common locale for such seduction was the bath, where there was a perfectly innocent excuse to be seen in the nude. In the Mesopotamian tale of *Enlil and Ninlil*, the young goddess Ninlil used this very technique to seduce her future husband:

> At that time the maiden was advised by her own mother, Ninlil was advised by Nunbaršegunu: "The river is holy, woman! The river is holy – don't bathe in it! Ninlil, don't walk along the bank of the Idnunbirtum! His eye is bright, the lord's eye is bright, he will look at you! The Great Mountain, Father Enlil – his eye is bright, he will look at you! The shepherd who decides all destinies – his eye is bright, he will look at you! Straight away he will want to have intercourse, he will want to kiss! He will be happy to pour lusty semen into the womb!" . . . The woman bathed in the holy river. As Ninlil walked along the bank of the Idnunbirtum, his eye was bright, the lord's eye was bright, he looked at her.[54]

This particular myth brings up an interesting controversy in ANE studies. As the tale progresses, Enlil does, in fact, ask Ninlil for sex. She refuses, claiming

---

[53] Scurlock 2014: 103, with references.   [54] *Enlil and Ninlil*. ETCSL translation: t.1.2.1.

that "My vagina is small, it does not know pregnancy. My lips are young, they do not know kissing." Plus, what would her friends say? In the end, they have sex, Ninlil gets pregnant, and Enlil is banished from the city. Ninlil chases after him. At each new city Enlil disguises himself to avoid Ninlil; in each city Ninlil recognized her man and has sex with him again. In the end she winds up pregnant with four children and the couple marries. The most common interpretation of this myth is that Enlil raped Ninlil. Four times.

> The only Old Babylonian myths with Enlil as their protagonist highlight the sexual tensions underlying his relationship with Ninlil. In both *Enlil and Ninlil* and *Enlil and Sud*, agricultural prosperity is shown as ultimately following from the sexual abuse of Ninlil by her husband. This is most apparent in *Enlil and Ninlil*. Enlil rapes Ninlil. Banished from Nippur for his crime, he thrice seduces her by deceit.[55]

This interpretation is predicated on the idea that females have no sexual agency. But if we consider that females in the ANE had what might be termed a more "sex-positive" attitude, we might instead read this narrative as a story where Ninlil using her sexual allure seduces the man of her heart and successfully wins her man.[56]

Seduction need not only be for love or sexual pleasure, though: Females could also use their sexuality to manipulate males. In the Hurrian *Song of Ḫedammu* in a similar bath scene the Ištar-like goddess Šauška seduces her brother Teššub's enemy (§§11.2 and 16.2)

> Šauška went to the bath house. She went there to wash herself … She anointed herself with fine, perfumed oil. She adorned herself. And (qualities which arouse) love ran after her like puppies. … Šauška said to Ḫedammu: "Come up again. Come from the strong waters." … Šauška holds out her naked members toward Ḫedammu. Ḫedammu sees the beautiful goddess, and his penis springs forth. His penis impregnates.[57]

The theme of the erotic female seducing and manipulating a man gets a comical twist in Tablet 4 of the Ugaritic *Ba'al Cycle*. Here the up-and-coming young god Ba'al wants to have a palace/temple built in his honor. To do so requires the approval of the family patriarch, the high god El. At first Ba'al tries to get his friend Anat, El's daughter, to intervene on his behalf. But Anat notoriously lacks diplomacy and threatens to beat El senseless if he does not give her what she wants. Take Two: Ba'al and Anat ask El's wife Athirat to speak with Father El. The mother goddess had been doing the

---

[55] Jones 2003: 299. See also Cooper 1980: 180. [56] Budin 2024: 124–125.
[57] Hoffner 1998: 54–55, excerpted and slightly adapted.

laundry when the young deities arrive, but she leaves her chores and visits her husband:

> She comes to the mountain of El and enters
> The tent of the king, the Father of Years.
> At the feet of El she bows down and falls,
> Prostrates herself and honors him.
> There El perceives her,
> He breaks into a smile and laughs.
> His feet on the footstool he stamps,
> And twirls his fingers.
> ...
> "Why has Lady Athirat of the Sea arrived?
> Why has the Creatrix of the deities come?
> Are you very hungry, having traveled.
> Or are you very thirsty, having journeyed?
> ...
> Or does the 'hand'[58] of El the King excite you,
> The love of the Bull arouse you?"[59]

So rather than a lovely young goddess seducing the male with a glimpse of her naked wet body, a middle-aged housewife goddess leaves her laundry to plead with an aging patriarch who is hoping that the missus came by for an afternoon tryst. On the one hand we might read this as a comic inversion of a standard Near Eastern literary trope. On the other hand, it may in fact reveal a slice of normal domestic life: Even the married old folks still enjoyed the sexual elements in their lives.

The use of feminine allure to seduce and manipulate males also appears in the Bible, where there is rather little reference to the more positive aspects of female sexuality. Even so, even in these episodes there is a focus on the maintenance of law and social order, as the women involved are actively trying to fulfill the dictates of Levirate marriage, whereby the widow of a man who died without a child must marry and produce a son with the dead man's closest male relative. The most positive example of such behavior comes from Ruth. As with other seductive females in the ANE, Ruth initiates the relationship by catching the eye of her target, her kinsman Boaz. As she suggests to her mother-in-law: "Let me go to the field and glean among the ears of grain, behind someone in whose sight I may find favor" (Ruth 2:2). Having caught Boaz's eye and established a rapport (3:7), "When Boaz had eaten and drunk, and he was in a contented mood, he went to lie down at the end of the heap of grain. Then she came

---

[58] "Hand" is a euphemism for "penis." See Paul 2002: 490–491.
[59] CAT 1.4, Column IV, ll. 31–51, excerpted. Smith in Parker 1997: 127.

stealthily and uncovered his feet, and lay down." When he wakes up and asks her who she is, she replies, "I am Ruth, your servant; spread your cloak over your servant." It seems innocent enough. But if we were to read with an eye towards euphemism, we might wonder if the "feet" Ruth uncovers were actually his penis, with the request to be covered by a cloak a reference to sharing a bed/sleeping together. By the end of the book, the wealthy Boaz is seeking the hand of the young widow in marriage.

A more ambivalent seduction occurs in Genesis 38, when another young widow – Tamar – needs to become impregnated by a close male relative of her dead husband Er, a need complicated by the fact that both Er and his brother, Tamar's second husband Onan, died on their wedding night. Her father-in-law Judah was thus understandably concerned about handing over his final son Shelah. Needing to provide an heir for her dead husband(s), Tamar disguised herself as a prostitute and waited for Judah by the side of the road:

> When Judah saw her, he thought her to be a prostitute, for she had covered her face. He went over to her at the roadside and said, "Come, let me come into you," for he did not know that she was his daughter-in-law. (Genesis 38:15–16)

Tamar claims to charge him a kid from his flock, holding onto his staff and ring until payment can be made. Then she disappears, keeping the ring and staff until it is time to reveal the father of her unborn child(ren). By seducing her father-in-law she manages to provide the son (twin sons, actually) required of her for her dead husbands. It is perhaps a bit amusing that when the family members of Ruth and Boaz bless the new couple, they state, "And through the children that the LORD will give you by this young woman, may your house be like the house of Perez, whom Tamar bore to Judah!" (Ruth 4:12).

The KAR.KID/*Harīmtu*

While originally translated as "prostitute," the Akkadian word *harīmtu* (Sumerian KAR.KID) is now understood to be a woman without a father or a husband (i.e. not under patriarchal authority).[60] As she was neither a wife nor expected to be a wife, she was the one category of woman in Mesopotamia who was free to engage in sexuality outside the confines of marriage. Thus it was Šamhat the *harīmtu* who seduced Enkidu in the *Epic of Gilgameš* – as a *harīmtu* she was the only woman around who could go have sex (and a lot of it – seven days' worth) with a stranger. As with every other *harīmtu* in the sources, there is no evidence whatsoever that she was paid for this.

---

[60] Budin 2021: chapter 2; Assante 1998.

Rather, the *harīmātu* (plural) were what we might call sexually liberated – and from a male perspective sexually available – women. They are often associated with the tavern, where people went to enjoy life, company, and beer. Even the goddess Inana, in a hymn of self-praise, declares:

> When I sit by the gate of the tavern, I am a KAR.KID familiar with the penis; the friend of a man, the girlfriend of a woman.

Such women could engage in social and sexual relations as they pleased, often in close, monogamous relationships. In point of fact, the children they bore to their lovers could legally be accepted as the father's official heir (indicating that the father's identity was not at all in dispute). Thus §27 of the Mesopotamian Law Code of Lipit-Ištar (c. 1930 BCE) states:

> If a man's spouse does not bear him a son and a KAR.KID from the street does bear him a son: He shall give grain rations, oil rations, and wool rations to the KAR.KID. The son whom the KAR.KID bears him is his heir. As long as his spouse is living, the KAR.KID shall not reside in the house with the first-spouse.[61]

There is no indication that such women were disreputable (although there *was* concern that they might displace a wife in a husband's affections).[62] In fact, the data indicate that they were placed in positions of authority in all-female households (tending to widowed mothers or fatherless siblings). Thus a last will from the Syrian city of Emar declares:

> [Bef]ore Šaḫurunuwa, son of Šarri-Kušuḫ, king of Ka[rkemi]š, Ḫaya, son of Ipqi-Dagan, has established this contract regarding his household.
> He has established his daughter Dada, the *harīmtu*, as father and mother of the household.
> (So speaks Ḫaya): "I have bestowed upon my daughter Dada a bed with its sheets, ... and a bronze headboard that covered the top (of the bed); these objects as well as two slaves, Au-milki and Ašti- ...
> I have adopted as sons my two daughters Dagan-niwari and Abi-qiri.[63]
> I have given Dagan-niwari as wife to Alal-abu. If [Dagan-niwari does not bear offspring], Alal-abu shall take another wife.
> May my daughters honor their father and mother Dada. If anyone of my daughters decides not to honor Dada, their father and mother, [she will not have the right] to her portion of the inheritance. May she take her clothing from the chair and go wherever she wishes. If they honor their father and mother, when (Dada) di[es] my two daughters will acquire my property and divide up the household and all my possessions equally.[64]

---

[61] Translation by Roth 2014: 150, slightly adapted.   [62] Roth 2006: 35.
[63] For the adopting of daughters as sons, and making daughters fathers and mothers, see Budin 2023: 227–231, with further citations.
[64] Emar 6 31. Translation: Justel 2014: 131.

There is no evidence that sex was ever exchanged for money (or comparable goods) in the Bronze Age in the Near East, what we would call "prostitution." Rather, there were women who did not have to reserve their sexuality for a patrilineal household and thus could date and have extramarital sex. The presence of such women may have actually *precluded* the need for prostitution.

Male Sexuality

Male Enjoyment

To judge from the mythological narratives, males were quite fond of sex, and they were utterly phallocentric about it. In point of fact, the Sumerian word for sexual intercourse is ĜEŠ.DU(G), formed by the signs ĜEŠ$_3$, "penis," and DUG$_4$, "to speak"; combined they have the meaning "to pour out," thus "to inseminate," thus "to make love to." The ĜEŠ.DUG verb was typically followed in the Sumerian literature by the verb NE SUB, "to kiss." The fact that the (typically male) lover "NE SUB-ed" his beloved only after he "ĜEŠ.DUG-ed" her may have a lot to say about the Mesopotamian male construct of foreplay.[65]

It is clear from the texts that ANE males used their penises a lot in sex, and they were not always entirely discriminating in their actions. In the Sumerian tale *Enki and Ninhursag* the Mesopotamian god of fresh water (which was also the word for semen – A) is trying to have sex with the goddess Nintur:

> Enki, the wise one,
> Toward Nintur, the country's mother,
> Was digging his phallus into the levee,
> Plunging his phallus into the canebreak.
> The august one, for her part,
> Pulled his phallus aside and cried out:
> "No man take me in the marsh!"[66]

Enki really did not even need a partner. As we read in *Enki and the World Order* (ll. 250–265):

> After he had turned his gaze from there, after father Enki had lifted his eyes across the Euphrates, he stood up full of lust like a rampant bull, lifted his penis, ejaculated and filled the Euphrates with flowing water. ... The Tigris ... at his side like a rampant bull. By lifting his penis, he brought a bridal gift. The Tigris rejoiced in its heart like a great wild bull, when it was born .... It brought water, flowing water indeed: its wine will be sweet. It brought barley, mottled barley indeed: The people will eat it. It filled the E-kur, the house of Enlil, with all sorts of things.[67]

---

[65] Zsolnay 2014: 279; Wiggermann 2010: 411. [66] Jacobsen 1987: 191.
[67] Black et al. 2004: 220–221.

In Tablet 5 of the Ugaritic *Ba'al Cycle*, on his way literally to confront Death, the storm god Ba'al stops to have a dalliance with a cow:

> Mightiest Ba'al hears;
> He makes love with a heifer in the outback,
> A cow in a field of Death's realm.
> He lies with her seventy times seven,
> Mounts eighty times eight;
> She conceives and bears a boy.[68]

We even read in the *Hittite Laws* that while bestiality was punishable by death for sex with cows, sheep, pigs, and dogs, it was not a punishable offence for an actual mortal man (not a deity) to have sex with a horse or a mule (see the section on "Bestiality").

In general, though, males/gods did generally prefer to have sex with more anthropomorphic females. We already saw how the deity-of-a-certain-age El was lustful for his wife Athirat (also of a certain age). But this did not stop him from engaging in some more fantasy-oriented endeavors. Thus in the Ugaritic tale *Birth of the Gracious Gods*:

> El's "hand" grows long as the sea,
> El's "hand" as the ocean.
> . . .
> El charms the pair of maids.
> If the maiden pair cries out:
> "O husband! husband!
> Lowered is your scepter,
> Generous the 'staff' in your hand."
> . . .
> He bows down to kiss their lips,
> Ah! their lips are sweet,
> Sweet as succulent fruit.
> In kissing, conception,
> In embracing, pregnant heat.
> The two travail and give birth
> to the gods Dawn and Dusk.[69]

Sometimes the aging patriarch in question might lose some control of the situation. Consider, for example, the rather comic case of biblical Jacob, his two wives, and their two servants (Genesis 30). First, Jacob works for seven years to win the hand of Rachel, only to be tricked at the last moment and receives her older sister Leah instead. Then he has to work for an additional seven years to

---

[68] Parker 1997: 148. [69] Lewis in Parker 1997: 210–213.

win Rachel. Both sisters bring female slaves into the household. Jacob has sons with Leah, but Rachel is barren. So Rachel gives Jacob her slave Bilhah to have sex with and thus produce children (really: sons) on her behalf. Then when Leah stops having children, she tells Jacob to have sex with her slave Zilpah, leading to more sons. Then Rachel gets some fertility-enhancing drugs from Leah's son in exchange for letting Leah have sex with Jacob that night. *Both* Rachel and Leah wind up pregnant, as do *both* Bilhah and Zilpah. And so on. Between the four women Jacob had twelve sons and one daughter – Dinah. Throughout, Jacob demonstrates very little agency or enjoyment.

Fertility

As already noted a few times in this Element, it was males who were associated with fertility in the ancient world. Male sexuality was therefore heavily intertwined with notions of fertility and reproduction. As we saw with Enki, his semen creating and filling the Tigris River gave rise to water, wine, and barley (and thus beer). When a god had sex with goddess or bovine, the result was inevitably progeny.

The notion of (divine) male potency was so strong, in fact, that in the mythologies of Mesopotamia, Anatolia, and even Egypt there were tales of male gods who got pregnant from ingesting semen, sometimes their own. In the Mesopotamian tale of *Enki and Ninhursag* Enki has sex with so many of his female descendants (thus impregnating them with the next generation he'll seduce) the mother goddess Ninhursag finally gives him a taste of his own medicine, tricks him into eating his own semen, and gets him pregnant with a multiplicity of vegetation deities. By contrast, in the Anatolian *Song of Kumarbi*, the god Kumarbi becomes pregnant after biting off the loins of the sky-deity Anu, whom he is attempting to overthrow.

> Kumarbi bit Anu's loins, and his "manhood" united with Kumarbi's insides like bronze. When Kumarbi had swallowed the "manhood" of Anu, he rejoiced and laughed out loud. Anu turned around and spoke to Kumarbi: "Are you rejoicing within yourself because you have swallowed my manhood?
>
> "Stop rejoicing within yourself! I have placed inside you a burden. First, I have impregnated you with the noble Storm God. Second, I have impregnated you with the irresistible Aranzah River. Third, I have impregnated you with the noble Tasmisu. And two additional terrible gods I have placed inside you as burdens. In the future you will end up striking the boulders of Mount Tassa with your head!"[70]

---

[70] Hoffner 1998: 42–43.

Gods could get pregnant, but it inevitably ended badly because males are not supposed to get pregnant, and ultimately they do not have the means to give birth.

The penis as the locus of fertility is not exclusively a literary/mythological construct: It applies to mortal males as well. In Anatolia, as a matter of fact, there are texts that refer to the penis as the "wooden weapon" that brings abundance and prosperity. In the *Propitiation Ritual for the King's Sister Ziplantawiya* (CTH 443.A §8), King Tudhaliya I (or II) is blessed:

> We brought the statues to exactly their place. They lined them up on another rock. The container of dough where the honey was poured, she sets it on the rock. She breaks up 3 thick breads. She libates wine. She speak as follows, "As this rock is everlasting, may the lord, his wife, and his children likewise be everlasting. Let his weapon (TUKUL-*šu*) be pointing forth." They offer a *tūruppa*-bread with wine.[71]

Likewise, the *Daily Prayer to Telipinu* has as a blessing:

> Keep giving to them male children, female children, grandchildren, and great-grandchildren. Keep giving them assent and obedience. Keep giving them flourishing of grain, grapes, cattle, sheep, and people. Keep giving them the powerful divine weapon ($^{d.giš}$TUKUL-*in*) of a man pointed straight ahead.[72]

The weapon (TUKUL), clearly both divine and wooden in the second example (the determinative ^{d} means divine, while the determinative ^{giš} means wooden), is directly linked with the male subject in both texts and appears alongside references to fertility and abundance. Rather than warfare, that "weapon" sticking out straight ahead is associated with progeny (children and grandchildren), the flourishing of animals and plant life, and longevity. As Mary Backvarova put it, "The reference to the king's 'weapon pointing forth' has an obvious double meaning, as weapon and vigorous phallus producing progeny."[73]

Love Sickness

Love sickness (*muruṣ rami* in Akkadian) was regarded as an actual ailment in the Mesopotamian medical texts, which dutifully recorded symptoms, prognoses, and even possible cures. Thus we read for both males and females that:

> If he continually flutters about, he is continually insolent, he continually talks with himself (and) he continually laughs for no reason, he is sick with love sickness; it is the same for a man and a woman. If depression continually falls upon him, his breath is continually short, he eats bread (and) drinks water/

---

[71] Bachvarova 2017: 90.   [72] Bachvarova 2017: 90.   [73] Bachvarova 2017: 90.

beer but it does not agree with him, he says, "Ua, my heart!" and he is dejected, he is sick with love sickness; it is the same for a man and a woman.[74]

Since approximately 2250 BCE spells existed to solve the problem of unrequited love, aka love charms, which were for both males and females.[75] Such rituals included both an incantation and ritual actions to bind the reluctant beloved. An incantation for a woman desiring a man declares:

> I have hit you on the head, I have driven you out of your mind!
> Set your thinking to my thinking,
> Set your reason to my reason!
> I hold you in restraint, as Ištar held Dumuzi,
> (As) liquor binds him who drinks her.
> I have bound you with my mouth for breaths,
> With my vulva for urination,
> With my mouth for spitting,
> With my vulva for urination.
> May no rival come to you!
> Dog is crouching, pig is crouching,
> You too keep crouching on my thighs![76]

Love sickness also appears in the Bible. In 2 Samuel 13, in King David's household, we read how:

> David's son Absalom had a beautiful sister whose name was Tamar; and David's son Amnon fell in love with her. Amnon was so tormented that he made himself ill because of his sister Tamar, for she was a virgin and it seemed impossible to Amnon to do anything to her.

Rather than resorting to magic or other interventions, Amnon raped his half-sister.

Infertility

Barrenness

In many ways the real world was a bit more like the Bible than a hymn to Inana: Sex was supposed to lead to pregnancy and progeny. It was problematic if it did not. In point of fact, the inability to have children was considered so dire in the ANE that it formed part of some of those curses mentioned previously. When making their oath of loyalty to the Hittite king and queen soldiers had to declare:

> Whoever should transgress these oaths by undertaking evil against the king and queen or against the royal princes – let the oaths of the gods on that

---

[74] Scurlock 2014: 106.   [75] Leick 1994: 194–195.   [76] Foster 1993: 141.

account likewise destroy his future! Let his wife bear neither male nor female children!⁷⁷

Much nonfictional sexual intercourse took place within the confines of marriage for the express purpose of producing children (although, as we saw with that blessing from Inana, it was totally acceptable to enjoy the process). If a couple was infertile, a standard recourse was for the husband to get a second/another wife. This was written into legal documents. Thus a marriage contract between Zunzuri and Idatti from the city of Alalakh in Syria was quite clear on the rules and regulations of marriage and offspring (ll. 2–9):

> From this day, before [Niqmepa the king:]
> The daughter of Ilimili,
> Zunzuri, Idat[ti]
> Has taken for a wife.
> Two hundred shekels of silver and thirty shekels of gold
> He has given as a bride price.
> [I]f she has not given birth after seven years,
> He may take a second wife.⁷⁸

In Mesopotamia, the *Law Code of Hammurabi* (§§144–147) regulates the process by which a female category of chaste cult functionary called the *nadītu* (literally: "fallow") – who in some contexts were allowed to marry but *not* allowed to reproduce/have children – provide a *šugītu* (a kind of concubine) to their husbands for the bearing of children. According to the final statute, "If she [the *šugītu*] does not bear children, her mistress may sell her."⁷⁹

Similar methods appear in the Bible, with the most famous example perhaps being that of Abram, Sarai, and Hagar (Genesis 16:1–4):

> Abram's wife Sarai had borne him no children. Now she had an Egyptian slave-girl whose name was Hagar, and she said to Abram, "You see that the LORD has not allowed me to bear a child. Take my slave-girl; perhaps I shall found a family through her." Abram agreed to what his wife said; so Sarai, Abram's wife, brought her slave-girl, Hagar the Egyptian, and gave her to her husband Abram as a wife/concubine ... He lay with Hagar and she conceived.

Later Sarai, now become Sarah, conceives Isaac (and Hagar and her son Ismael are banished to the desert). This is another common motif in the Bible, whereby barrenness is seen as having been sent by God so that he might later intervene and bless the woman with a late-born son. A similar example is Hannah in 1 Samuel 1, where Hannah only conceives after vowing to dedicate her eventual

---

⁷⁷ Beckman 2016: 320, with further citations.   ⁷⁸ AT 93. Hess 2003: 252.
⁷⁹ Roth 2014: 154.

son to God as a nazirite. Several means of dealing with female barrenness appear in the tale of Rachel, Leah, and Jacob in Genesis 30:

> When Rachel saw that she bore Jacob no children, she envied her sister; and she said to Jacob, "Give me children or I shall die!" Jacob became very angry with Rachel and said, "Am I in the place of God, who has withheld from you the fruit of your womb?" Then she said, "Here is my maid Bilhah; go in to her that she may bear upon my knees and that I too may have children through her." ... In the days of wheat harvest Reuben went and found mandrakes in the field, and brought them to his mother Leah. Then Rachel said to Leah, "Please give me some of your son's mandrakes." ... Then God remembered Rachel, and God heeded her and opened her womb. She conceived and bore a son.

Here we see the use of a replacement female body, use of medicinal herbs (mandrake), and finally divine intervention from a paternal deity.

One point that is very much worth noting is that wives were not necessarily abandoned because of barrenness. Slaves and "handmaidens" were, of course, treated like movable property, but both the legal texts and the literature indicate that husbands generally preferred to keep their wives, presumably out of love. Abraham never abandons Sarah. Genesis 29:30 is quite clear that "Jacob loved Rachel more than Leah," even though the latter bore him far more sons. And Hannah's husband would console his barren wife (1 Samuel 1:8): "Hannah, why do you weep? Why do you not eat? Why is your heart sad? Am I not more to you than ten sons?" Love does appear to have been an important aspect of marriage. But this never stopped the husbands from getting that second wife.

Impotence

Sometimes it was not the wife who was barren: Infertility could also come from the male side. And so our texts from the ANE have numerous remedies both medical and magical, often both at once. For the most part, they seem to deal specifically with impotence.

From Mesopotamia and Anatolia we have the ŠÀ.ZI.GA, or "rising of the 'heart'" texts.[80] There is evidence that they date back to Old Babylonian times (written in Sumerian), but they are best known from the Middle Babylonian period and continued in use into the fourth century BCE, now written in Akkadian. These collections of incantations and medical recipes existed to allow a man to feel desire for a woman, have an erection, and be able to maintain that erection during intercourse. Fertility was at best an afterthought, perhaps because it was assumed that successful intercourse

---

[80] "Heart" is a euphemism for "penis."

Sex and Sexuality in the Ancient Near East 35

would solve the fertility problem. From a medicinal perspective therapy might include rubbing the penis and lower body with an ointment made of plant oil and iron. Other concoctions were made with animal parts, preferably those engaged in mating or of known sexual potency. Thus the saliva of aroused animals; dried, copulating lizards; stag penis; or hair from a copulating ox (without any description about how one was supposed to go about getting that particular item).[81] More psychological aspects involved women "talking dirty" to their men, sometimes with props. Finally, deities such as Ištar, Išḫara, or even Marduk-Asalluḫi might be invoked. And so:

> Incantation: "Roar on me! Roar on me! Rear up! Rear up!
> Roar on me like a stag! Rear up like a wild bull!
> Together with you, may a lion rear up!
> Together with you, may a wolf rear up!
> Together with you, may a snake rear up!
> All the muscles of your limbs, your sperm . . .
> . . .
> May your penis, which satisfies . . . be compact! Do not . . .
> May my vulva devour your . . . penis!
> At the command of Kanisurra and Išḫara, patron goddess of love." Incantation.
> Its ritual: You pulverize magnetite, you mix it with oil from the alabastron,
> You recite the incantation seven times over it; you apply it to his navel;
> You pulverize iron, you mix it with oil from the alabastron, you recite the incantation seven times over it,
> You apply it to the woman's navel; the man and the woman will find relief together.[82]

Another example:

> Incantation: "Have sex! May you not be afraid!
> Rise! May you not be afflicted!
> At the command of Ištar, Šamaš, Ea, and Asalluḫi,
> The incantation of Ištar, patron of love." Incantation formula.
> Its ritual: Hair of a reared-up buck, the "something little" of its penis,
> . . . wool of a reared-up ram, red wool . . .
> You bind them around his waist, you libate pure water, you recite the incantation seven times.[83]

There is a logic to the magic and the medicine. In the first example, the man is anointed with an ointment containing magnetite, while the woman is anointed with iron oil. Obviously, this should pull them together. In the latter example, the man has parts of sexually aroused male animals – buck and ram – tied around his waist, sending the animals' libido to where the man needs it most. While all this is happening, his partner calls for sex. Assuming the man does not

---

[81] Biggs 2002: 76. [82] Zisa 2021: 263, slightly adapted. [83] Zisa 2021: 291.

get performance anxiety at the mention of Ištar or Išḫara, all should work out well.

From Anatolia we have the Hittite text known as *Paškuwatti's Ritual against Sexual Impotence*, composed in the Middle Hittite period but known from a single tablet dating to the thirteenth century BCE.[84] Based on the textual data, the purpose of this ritual performed by the woman Paškuwatti of Arzawa before the goddess Uliliyassi is to deal with a man who "has no reproductive power or is not a man vis-à-vis a woman."[85] This is accomplished by invoking the goddess in the steppe with bread rituals while removing the patient's femininity and replacing it with masculinity. The relevant portions of the text are:

> 1) Thus Paškuwatti, the Arzawa woman, who lives in Parassa. If some man has no reproductive power or is not a man vis-à-vis a woman.
> 2) I make offerings to Uliliyassi on his behalf and entreat her for three days...
> 4) I tie them (gates of reeds) together with red and white wool. I place a spindle and a distaff in the patient's [hand], and he comes under the gates. When he steps forward through the gates, I take the spindle and distaff away from him. I give him a bow (and) arrows, and say to him all the while: "I have just taken femininity away from you and given you masculinity in return. You have cast off the behavior expected [of women]; [you have taken] to yourself the behavior expected of men ....
> ...
> 8) (Speaking to the goddess) "Come to this man! You are his "wife of children" for him! So look after him! Turn to him [in favor] and speak to him! Turn your maidservant (the man's wife) over to him, and he will become a yoke. Let him take his wife and produce for himself sons and daughters!"[86]

The evidence from the text itself reveals that procreation is what is at issue, as the rite begins with a reference to a man with no reproductive power and continues and ends with a repeated reference to that man taking his wife and producing for himself sons and daughters. One way or another, reproduction is at issue.

Even our comparably limited corpus from Ugarit has a ritual for curing impotence. Text RIH 78/20 cites sorcery for the "pain of your rod":

> This recitation casts out the tormentors of a young man:
> The pain of your rod it has banished,
> The producers of the pain of your rod.
> It goes forth at the voice of the *ta'iyu* priest

---

[84] Hoffner 1987: 280.   [85] Hoffner 1987: 277.
[86] Hoffner 1987: 277–278. The final line about producing sons and daughters is repeated in section 14.

> Like smoke from a window,
> Like a serpent from a pillar,
> Like mountain goats to a summit,
> Like lions to a lair.
> The rod has recovered.
> ...
> Then, as for the sorcerers, the tormentors,
> Ḥôranu will drive them out,
> Even the companions and the "lads of wisdom" he will drive out for you.
> With respect to heat, do not sag,
> May your tongue not stutter,
> May your canal not be decanalized.
> ...
> For the man, descend from the rod to the earth, O flow;
> For the son of man, from illness he is delivered.[87]

Sometimes impotence simply comes from being old. One answer, thought the ancients, was to get a younger partner. A Sumerian folk tale known as "The Old Man and the Young Girl" tells the story of a decrepit old man who goes to the king to get help for his various bodily afflictions (excerpted):

> I was a youth, but now my luck, my strength, my personal god, and my youthful vigor have left my loins like an exhausted ass.
> My black mountain has produced white gypsum (i.e. my hair has turned white)
> My "mongoose" which used to eat strong smelling things does not stretch its neck towards butter and beer.
> My urine used to flow in a strong torrent, but now you flee from my wind.[88]

When the king askes for advice, his council advises:

> My king, suppose that the old man took a young girl as wife.
> In the rest of his days – as long as they last, as long as they are – the old man will regain his youthful vigor, and the young girl will become a mature woman.[89]

The king finds this reasonable and offers a girl to the old man, telling her, "After I have given him to you, he will lie in your lap like a young man."[90] The tale is generally understood to be a comedy.

The biblical authors were perhaps a tad more realistic. When King David had similar issues towards the end of his reign (1 Kings 1:1–4):

> King David was now old, advanced in years; and though they covered him with bedclothes, he never felt warm. His courtiers said to him, "Let a young

---

[87] Pardee 2002: 160–161, excerpted. [88] Alster 1975: 93. [89] Alster 1975: 93.
[90] Alster 1975: 93.

virgin be sought for my lord the king, to wait upon your majesty and be his attendant, and let her lie in your bosom, and my lord the king will be warm." So they looked for a beautiful girl throughout the territory of Israel. They found Abishag the Shunammite and brought her to the king. The girl was exceedingly beautiful. She became the king's attendant and waited upon him; but the king was not intimate with her.

Sexual Orientation

The Foucauldian Disclaimer

Whenever Theory-informed scholars of antiquity attempt to deal with the matter of ancient sexuality, they oblige themselves to go through a torturous verbal rigmarole wherein they explain that the ancients did not actually have sexuality, and they most assuredly did not have notions of heterosexuality or homosexuality, which are exclusively modern, Western constructs. For example: "[H]eterosexuality is not immutable, it is a modern concept, one that was invented by the West to make sense of yet another Western construct, i.e. homosexuality."[91] In so doing, the Theory-informed scholars of antiquity are paying homage to Michel Foucault, who argued that heterosexual and homosexual identity did not exist before the early modern age in the European context.

This is absurd for a few reasons. To begin, Foucault was not an ancient historian, so he is not a reliable source on ancient things, including sexuality. Even with that, modern scholars have rather missed the point here. What Foucault argued was that sexuality (hetero- or homo-) was not a category of *self-identification* before the modern era. In modern times a gay man might identify as gay in the same breath as identifying as being British, a Scorpio, or Gen X. We now think of ourselves in terms of sexual identity in ways that we did not previously.

Furthermore, some Theory-informed scholars of antiquity claim that heterosexuality and homosexuality did not exist because there were no words for them. As Camille Paglia noted in her tirade over this recent trend, "This is just absurd: it's like Arctic explorers coming upon penguins for the first time and informing them, 'I'm sorry, you did not exist before we named you.'"[92] Also, this position is simply incorrect. For example, in the fourth-century BCE Platonic dialogue *Symposion*, in the comic speech of Aristophanes, we come across mention of men who "love men and enjoy lying with men and being embraced by men" just as we find "women who are oriented towards women" (*Symposion* 191e). Plato did not have a specific word for either group, but the

---
[91] Dowson 2008: 27. [92] Paglia 1991: 145.

concept of same-sex love is explicit. So, yes, the ancients *did* understand that human beings were sexually aroused by different categories of human beings – what we might now call "sexual orientation."

The ancients knew of sexual orientation, including heterosexuality, homosexuality, and bisexuality. This is not an anachronism.

Heterosexuality

The inhabitants of the ANE were what we would call "heteronormative." This fact has nothing to do with matters of desire or sexual orientation or gender identity. It has everything to do with the structure of ANE society, which was based on the family. Families need children for labor and to continue to exist, and the only way to create children was and is via heterosexual intercourse. There is no evidence that the ancients thought of themselves as heteronormative, or even specifically heterosexual, just as they did not think of themselves as pagan. To do so would have required some other category, which they did not recognize, at least not as presented in their texts and images. Rather, heteronormativity expresses in the repeated references to heterosexual relationships in all genres of literature and art and the extreme paucity of references to homosexuality (see below). All the law codes, the wisdom literature, the love songs, the narratives are filled with the expression and regulation of heterosexual relationships: engagement and dowries and marriage and adultery and what makes a good wife and how to be a good husband; families with mothers and fathers and how they pass on inheritance to their children and others; what constitutes adultery and rape and how to distinguish between the two;[93] the curing of sexual dysfunction with sexual partners of consistently the opposite sex;[94] hymns to a beloved who is consistently of the opposite sex;[95] lists of workers with families and assorted dependents, most showing men and women in heterosexual marriages and families, a few showing unmarried men and women, none showing same-sex couples; and so on.

As the poetry makes abundantly clear, heterosexual sex was thoroughly enjoyable. But apart from characters like Inana, it was consistently complicated by matters of reproduction, either the need to produce children or concerns about infertility. So, on the one hand, heterosexual intercourse was fun. On the other hand, it was *work* – a necessary task in the life of the ANE. One may recall the scene in the movie *Stargate* when James Spader's character is sitting and

---

[93] See usefully on these issues Roth 2014.
[94] On the ŠÀ.ZI.GA texts and the curing of erectile dysfunction in Mesopotamia, see the previous section on magico-medical texts and, further, Biggs 1967 and 2002 and, more recently, Zisa 2021.
[95] See Leick 1994.

chatting with a group of ancient Egyptian-like aliens (this makes sense in the movie) and one of them gestures to him and comments, "The husband doesn't do his job." The men find it funny that Spader is not having a lot of sex with his new wife but couch this in the very real terms of not doing his "job" as a husband: impregnating his wife. Spader, having clarified things with the young woman he had no idea he had married ("HUSBAND?????"), immediately gets to work. So while the residents of the ANE were far more open to the enjoyable aspects of sexuality than in some later, usually Christo-Muslim, societies, heterosexuality was often tinged with the shadow of reproduction – pillow talk followed by that rather unromantic question, "Are you pregnant yet?"

Homosexuality

References to homosexuality[96] are absurdly scarce in the ANE, far more than one would guess given how much controversy it generates in modern times. The ancients just do not seem to have given all that much thought to homosexuality, certainly less than we do. It definitely existed in the ANE: There are enough data to indicate that the ancients knew of it. It just did not come up all that often – one or two laws over the entire course of Mesopotamian legal history; a passing reference from Anatolia; a few omen texts. And what does exist concerns males only; nothing whatsoever is extant about lesbianism. To put it simply, when it comes to sex we have far more data pertaining to incest and bestiality than we do to homosexuality. Perhaps, being without offspring to be concerned about, the ancients simply felt that such relationships were none of their business.

This is not the common wisdom about ancient homosexuality in modern discourse, whether in academia or in popular culture. The general understanding now is that the ancients – with the possible exception of some Greeks and Romans – saw (male) homosexuality as a bad thing. Either it is a sinful, illegal act condemned by a deity (the biblical version) or it is problematic in society as it creates unstable hierarchies among men because it creates males who dominate other males. Neither understanding is particularly accurate. Let us consider them in reverse if chronological order.

Get the Foucault Out! On Foucault (Again)

Classicists tend to delve into Theory-oriented disciplines like feminist studies, gender studies, and queer studies before Assyriologists and Biblicists. As a result, there is a tendency in ANE studies to look at what the Greco-Romanists have

---

[96] Homosexuality in this section refers to male homosexuality. Unfortunately, we have nothing on lesbianism.

done in a new field as a starting point, applying their hypotheses and theories to their own data. Problems emerge when there is insufficient recognition of the fact that very different cultures and datasets are being considered, not to mention insufficient consideration of whether or not what the Classicists said was correct in the first place. This is a monumental problem in the study of ANE homosexuality because ANE scholars adopted whole-cloth the Classicist idea that penetrative sex is all about domination. The one who penetrates is the dominant, active partner, while the one who is penetrated is the subordinate, passive, innately "feminine/effeminate" partner. In Classics the paradigm was first construed by Kenneth Dover in his seminal book *Greek Homosexuality*, published in 1978. Here, in a section on "Dominant and Subordinate Roles," after a section on the humiliation of apparent prostitutes in vase painting he turns to relations between males.

> There seems little doubt that in Greek eyes the male who breaks the "rules" of legitimate eros detaches himself from the ranks of male citizenry and classifies himself with women and foreigners ... To choose to be treated as an object at the disposal of another was to resign one's own standing as a citizen ... it should become so when we recall circumstances in which homosexual anal penetration is treated neither as an expression of love nor as a response to the stimulus of beauty, *but as an aggressive act demonstrating the superiority of the active to the passive partner*.[97]

A major follower of Dover's turned out to be none other than Michel Foucault. In his *The Use of Pleasure* Foucault expanded Dover's theories to the rest of humanity, claiming:

> We have to recall a principle, which is doubtless not particular to Greek culture, but which assumed considerable importance within it and exercised a decisive authority in moral valuations. I am referring to the principle of isomorphism between sexual relations and social relations – always conceived in terms of the model act of penetration, assuming a polarity that opposed activity and passivity – were seen as being of the same type as the relationship between superior and a subordinate, an individual who dominates and one who is dominated, one who commands and one who complies, one who vanquishes and one who is vanquished. ... And this suggests that in sexual behavior there was one role that was intrinsically honorable and valorized without question: the one that consisted of being active, in dominating, in penetrating, in asserting one's superiority.[98]

As a result, Foucault convinced academia that homosexuality between males is all about penetration and domination where the dominator penetrated a submissive penetratee who was thus, specifically, *feminized* by the process.

---

[97] Dover 1978/1989: 103–104, excerpted. My emphasis. [98] Foucault 1985/1990: 215.

In reality, we have no data from the ANE that indicate any such "principle." What we actually get are cases like the following four omens from the seventh-century BCE omen series *Šumma ālu* ("If a City ..."):

> (CT 39 44:13) If a man penetrates his social peer via the buttocks/anus, that man will become foremost among his brothers and colleagues.
> (CT 39 45:32) If a man penetrates an *assinnu*, hardships will be unleashed from him.
> (CT 39 45:33) If a man penetrates a *girseqû*, for an entire year the deprivations which beset him will be kept away.
> (CT 39 45:34) If a man penetrates a male house[-born] slave, hardship will seize him.[99]

These four omens pertain to a man "penetrating" other men. In the first, it is a peer who is penetrated, specifically via the buttocks/anus. Thus, anal sex with a peer. In the other three, penetration (without reference to the body part entailed) occurs with an *assinnu* (a cult functionary of Ištar), a *girseqû* (a palace official), or a household slave. In the first three, the apodosis is beneficial: The penetrating man gets status, or at least dodges hardships. It is only the final apodosis that is negative: The man who penetrates a household male slave is beset with hardships. The fourth clearly upsets Foucault's "principle."

What we get in modern commentary, however, tries to bend the interpretation to follow the Foucauldian model. It is thus assumed that there is something "off" about the *assinnu* and *girseqû* – they are somehow not "real" men and thus being penetrated simply emphasizes their subordinate, feminine nature. To quote Ann Guinan, world authority on the sex omen texts:

> An *assinnu*, a character who appears in a variety of Mesopotamian sources, is a performer in an Ištar cult and is distinguished by dress, hairstyle, and female accoutrements. Variously a transvestite, a hermaphrodite, or eunuch, the *assinnu* is a transgressive figure of ambiguous or, perhaps, even mutable gender and overt sexual display. A *girseqû* has domestic duties associated with the palace or temple. Sexual relations with these partners represent dominance and gaining of power.[100]

But it is not at all clear that the *assinnu* has "mutable gender" or "overt sexual display."[101] Furthermore, other than running the palace it is difficult to see how the *girseqû* is supposed to be "effeminate." If having sex with either of

---

[99] Guinan 1997: 479.   [100] Guinan 1997: 469.
[101] There is actually a huge debate currently going on about this. See Budin 2023: 190–198 and Peled 2016: Chapter 3 for a starting point.

these men is beneficial, it is far from obvious that it has anything to do with their innate subordination or femininity. In fact, quite the opposite could be true.

As for the household slave, he most certainly *is* as subordinate as they come. Even so, having sex with him is a bad thing according to the fourth omen. Why? Again quoting Guinan, "Sexual relations with a slave born of the house are a type of encounter that is, perhaps, too close to home and this sexual involvement does not have a place in the social arena."[102] Said differently, one does not get machismo credit for actions that take place at home, shielded from the public eye. But this does not explain why the apodosis is specifically bad, rather than merely neutral (or positive, considering the reinforcement of the Foucauldian ideal).

And as for that peer in the first omen, the logic seems to be:

> Just as every man can be a penetrator, he can also be penetrated. The binary structures of gender asymmetry are located on the same male body. A male equal who chooses to be penetrated makes the somatic contradiction inherent in the logic of gender asymmetry all too close to becoming visible. His act threatens the logic of binary gender and undermines the terms of gender hierarchy on which social organization is predicated. Sex between male equals, which opens the possibility of reversible positions and the symmetrical deployment of the body, is a double annihilation of hierarchy.[103]

In this "annihilation of hierarchy" the first omen should, technically, lead to a negative outcome (the first three, really), just as the last omen should be positive, as the domination of the master over the slave reinforces hierarchy. Instead, male penetrative sex in the first three omens leads to positive outcomes, with the exception (the fourth omen) being if one has sex with a household slave. Based on the contrast with the first three omens, one might suggest that sex with one who is not merely a social inferior but one with no agency (a slave) – as in the fourth omen – is a form of rape, what the Greeks would have called an act of *hubris*. A man who commits *hubris* in his own household is indeed potentially in for a world of trouble.[104] So the problem with the fourth omen is not homosexuality, but rape. There is nothing wrong with homosexuality per se.

This exact same dynamic appears writ large in the Bible, specifically in Genesis 19 and Judges 19. The first is the well-known tale of Sodom and Gomorrah, wherein two angels disguised as mortal travelers accept hospitality with the (anti)hero Lot, then living in Sodom. That night the men of Sodom

---
[102] Guinan 1997: 469.
[103] Guinan, 1997: 470–471. As she restates in her 2022 publication, "Ominous ambiguity is also in play, as the logic of reversible position is embodied in every man" (Guinan 2022: 81).
[104] Budin 2023: 257.

surround the house demanding that the travelers be sent out so that the men might "know" them. Lot offered instead his virgin daughters, to no avail. In the end the angels blinded the mob. The second tells the story of an anonymous man of Ephraim who travels to Bethlehem in Judah to recover his secondary wife/concubine. After staying several days with his father-in-law he and the secondary wife traveled until they reached Gibeah in Benjaminite territory, where they were eventually taken in by a man also from Ephraim now residing in Gibeah. As was the case in Sodom, at night the men of the town came to the man's house demanding that he hand over the visitor so that they might "know" him. The host offered instead his virgin daughter and the man's secondary wife. The men refused. But when the husband threw the secondary wife out to them, the men gang-raped her until she died. This was then used as a reason for the men of the north to unite and fight a war against the Benjaminites and ultimately abduct their virgins.

Both tales relate how one or more male entities (man, angels) were threatened with rape when visiting unfamiliar territory. In both instances, their host, also a foreigner in the town, attempted to protect the guests by offering one or more virgin daughters to the gang of rapists, who declined. Even so, in the latter narrative it is a *woman* who is cast out, raped, and killed. It is likely that the matter of threatened rape in Genesis 19 and Judges 19 pertains to a biblical literary trope whereby rape leads to the destruction of the perpetrators (e.g. Genesis 34:25–29, 2 Samuel 13). The variation here is that the threatened victims are male. And, to repeat: *threatened*. No male–male sexual intercourse actually occurs in either Genesis 19 or Judges 19: both males and females (the daughters and concubine) are threatened, but it is *only* a female who is ever actually raped in any of the rape narratives.

Ironically, then, there is no actual homosexuality in either Genesis 19 or Judges 19. What is presented is not intercourse but (threatened) rape. Rape is its own category of sexuality and cannot be used as evidence for the social acceptability or morality of consensual forms of sexuality. Rape is independent of both homosexuality and heterosexuality.

Against the Law (?)

Two texts from Leviticus are important in the question of legality:[105]

> Leviticus 18:22: And with a male you shall not lie the lying down of a woman; it is *tô'ēbâ*.[106]

---

[105] Translations from Olyan 1994: 180.
[106] On *tô'ēbâ*, See Olyan 1994: 180, n. 3. The usual translation is "abomination," but one might also take it as "a sin highly offensive to a particular deity."

> Leviticus 20:13: And as for the man who lies with a male the lying down of a woman, they – the two of them – have committed a *tôʻēbâ*; they shall certainly be put to death; their blood is upon them.

These are the only two references to (male) homosexuality in the Hebrew Bible. Two things need to be kept in mind when considering them. First, more likely than not, what we actually have here is one law, not two. The laws in Leviticus 20 for the most part reduplicate the laws in Leviticus 18. So, for example, just before the bit about "lying with a man" in both texts we read:

> Leviticus 18:21: You shall not give any of your offspring to sacrifice them to Molech, and so profane the name of your God.
> Leviticus 20:2: Any Israelite or any foreigner residing in Israel who sacrifices any of his children to Molech is to be put to death. The members of the community are to stone him.

Basically, Leviticus 18 presents a list of things that are illegal – you may not lie with a man, sacrifice your children to Molech, have sex with an animal (more on this below), and so on. This list gets repeated in Leviticus 20, only this time with a reference to punishment, usually death. Same laws: expanded format. So, technically, the entire Hebrew Bible presents a total of one law prohibiting male homosexuality. For the record, this is in contrast to *numerous* prohibitions to all kinds of incest.

The second thing to keep in mind regarding Leviticus 18:22 and 20:13 is that "[t]hey are the only such laws in the Hebrew Bible: there is absolutely nothing analogous to them in the other Israelite collections mediated to us."[107] We have no idea where these laws came from. While there have been numerous speculations regarding purity violations, wasting male seed/sperm, and/or establishing Judean identity in the face of (presumably "perverted") Canaanites and/or Greeks/Romans, the fact is that we have *no idea* why this law exists. It is a wholly isolated law, and one with far less consequence in the Bible than, say, having sex with your mother-in-law or your wife when she is menstruating. The things that were actually important.

The only other law from the ANE that prohibits male homosexuality comes from the *Middle Assyrian Laws* (MAL).

> §20: If a man has sex with his peer (*tappāʼu*) (and) they prove the charges against him and find him guilty, they will have sex with him and turn him into/over to a *ša rēši*.[108]

The latter part of the punishment is open to debate. The standard understanding is that the man is castrated, with the *ša rēši* understood to be

---

[107] Olyan 1994: 181. [108] Guinan and Morris 2017: 169.

a eunuch. This is absolutely possible. However, there are some reasons to question this translation of *ša rēši*, and an alternative translation is that they turn the man *over to* a *ša rēši*, that is, deliver him to a high-ranking administrator.[109]

As is typical, this law is generally understood in terms of the Foucauldian dominant masculine versus passive feminine/effeminate paradigm. For one scholar, "Penetrating a *tappā'u* was tantamount to rape and deliberate disgrace, because the penetrating partner effects a change in the other partner's role from active (male) to passive (female)."[110] For another, "Either by word or by deed, one close associate has subordinated another – it is an infringement of masculine position or agency in a community of men who share the prerogatives of power. It is not hard to detect a sense of masculinity under threat in these legal texts."[111] And concerning the eventual punishment:

> This violent feminization of the *awīlu* offender clearly casts him forever out of his peer group and asserts a radical gender hierarchy between *awīlu* and criminal. The offender's altered position as the "other," a viable object of male predation, one who can never again penetrate, recovers and exaggerates the lost masculine status of the violated *awīlu*.[112]

However, it must be observed that there is no reference to force being used. The word *emūqamma* – "forcibly" – appears in the laws pertaining to adultery to distinguish between sex as adultery and sex as rape. This word does not appear in §20, and thus it appears that rape is *not* at issue. So whatever punishment accrues to the subject, it is not because of rape. Furthermore, there is no indication of who brings the matter to court (so to speak): That is, it is not stated that the *object* of the sexual encounter is prosecuting the man who penetrated him. This may also argue against the rape hypothesis, as there is no male accusing another male of violence.

Ultimately, like the biblical law(s), MAL §20 is unique in the Mesopotamian corpus, not just in the MAL but the *entire* corpus of Mesopotamian jurisprudence. In the absence of any comparable laws, it is impossible to hypothesize what it meant to the Assyrians who formulated it and possibly enforced it. But its uniqueness and narrow focus indicate quite a limited interest in homosexuality in Mesopotamia.

---

[109] Dalley 2001: 200. On the debate about the definition of *ša rēši*, see Budin 2023: 160–170, with further citations.
[110] Nissinen 1998: 26.   [111] Guinan and Morris 2017: 152.
[112] Assante 2017: 48. *Awīlu* means "man."

The Anatolians did not legislate on homosexuality at all. The closest we come is §189 of the *Hittite Laws*, which states:

> §189: If a man sins (sexually) with his own mother, it is an unpermitted sexual pairing (*ḫūrkil*).[113] If a man sins (sexually) with (his) daughter, it is an unpermitted sexual pairing. If a man sins (sexually) with (his) son, it is an unpermitted sexual pairing.[114]

The prohibition against having sex with one's own son is the closest we come to references to homosexuality among the Hittites, and as is clear from the rest of the law, this is a prohibition against incest, not homosexuality.

Heterosexuality is complicated by concerns over reproduction. Homosexuality is complicated by modern discourses about it. As noted previously, the joys of heterosexual sex in the real world are always tinged with concerns about fertility or the lack thereof. There are no such constraints with homosexuality – in the absence of children, property transfer, marriage contracts, and so on, it is a sexuality that can be based purely on affection and mutual pleasure. Homosexual sex is not work (except in the case of prostitution). But in modern discourse we often ignore the emotional aspects of (homosexual) sex, somehow refuse to consider that it can be an expression of love and affection, and regard it solely in terms of domination and criminality. The modern world really needs to reconsider how it looks at ancient homosexuality.

The Dark Side: Sexual Crimes
Adultery

The problem with seduction is that even married women can do it, and not necessarily with their husbands. Because of the patriarchal nature of ANE societies, where family property and family cult went through the male line, there was considerable concern about the sexual constancy of wives. As we shall see, there were numerous laws that dealt with adultery, with punishments for both male and female perpetrators (i.e. adulterous wives and the men they had sex with, *not* men who had sex outside of marriage). The narrative texts, however, tend only to recognize cases of married women having affairs. Perhaps we see a bit of (older) male insecurity in the fact that these tales tend to feature supposedly younger men.

One of the most famous examples is the biblical tale of Joseph and Potiphar's wife (Genesis 39):

---

[113] On this term see Hoffner 1973: 83–84. [114] Hoffner 1997: 149.

> Now Joseph was well-built and handsome, and after a while his master's wife took notice of Joseph and said, "Come to bed with me!" But he refused. ... "My master has withheld nothing from me except you, because you are his wife. How then could I do such a wicked thing and sin against God?" And though she spoke to Joseph day after day, he refused to go to bed with her or even be with her.
>
> One day he went into the house to attend to his duties, and none of the household servants was inside. She caught him by his cloak and said, "Come to bed with me!" But he left his cloak in her hand and ran out of the house ... She kept his cloak beside her until his master came home. Then she told him this story: "That Hebrew slave you brought us came to me to make sport of me. But as soon as I screamed for help, he left his cloak beside me and ran out of the house." When his master heard the story his wife told him, saying, "This is how your slave treated me," he burned with anger. Joseph's master took him and put him in prison, the place where the king's prisoners were confined.

A very similar tale comes from the Syro-Anatolian orbit, where a Hittite myth featuring deities with Canaanite names (Elkunirsa = El, and Ashertu = Asherah/Athirat) shows what happens when the queen of the gods makes advances at the young and handsome Ba'al:

> Elkunirsa looked at Ba'al and asked him, "Why have you come?" Ba'al said, "When I came into your house, Ashertu sent young women to me, saying, 'Come sleep with me.' I refused. Then she ... me and spoke thus, 'Stay behind me and I shall stay behind you. Else I shall press you down with my word and stab you with my ... .' That is why I have come, my father. I did not come to you in the person of a messenger; I myself have come to you. Ashertu is rejecting you, her own husband. Although she is your wife, she keeps sending to me: 'Sleep with me.'" Elkunira replied to Ba'al, "Go threaten her, Ashertu, my wife, and humble her!"[115]

The presence of these similar tales in the Levant may in fact derive from a prototype in Egypt. In the Egyptian *Tale of Two Brothers* two brothers – Anubis and Bata – live together along with Anubis's wife. One day when sent to fetch seed for planting in the fields, Bata comes across Anubis's wife in her chambers, having just finished adorning her hair. She approaches him, saying:

> "There is great manliness in you, for I have been observing your exertions daily." For it was her desire to know him sexually. She got up, seized him, and told him, "Come, let's spend for ourselves an hour in bed together. Such will be to your advantage, for I shall make fine clothes for you."[116]

---

[115] Hoffner 1998: 91, slightly adapted. [116] Simpson 1972: 95, adapted.

Bata refused and she accused him of attacking her, just as was the case for Joseph and Mrs. Potiphar. In the end Bata castrated himself to prove his loyalty to his brother, and the wife is killed and thrown to the dogs. So there are variations in the outcomes of these folk tales, but they all indicate a concern over uncontrollable female libido in marriage.

Concern about adultery also manifests in the various ANE law codes. A constant in Mesopotamian law is that wives were harshly punished for adultery, a fact that stands in stark contrast to the varying degrees of punishment (or not) faced by their paramours. In the *Laws of Ur-Nammu*, dating to c. 2100 BCE, it is declared that:

> §7: If the spouse of a young-man on her own initiative pursues a man and has sexual intercourse with him, they shall kill that woman; that male shall be given his freedom.[117]

§28 of the *Laws of Ešnunna* (c. 1800 BCE) equally calls for the death of a formally married wife, "the day she is seized in the lap of a man, she shall die, she will not live."[118] By contrast, the roughly contemporary *Laws of Hammurabi* (c. 1750) offer the choice of life or death to the accused woman's husband. §129 declares that:

> If the wife-of-a-man should be seized lying with another male: They will bind them and cast them into the water [the River Ordeal]; if the husband of the wife allows his wife to live, then the king will allow his slave [the paramour] to live.[119]

By the time of the Middle Assyrian Laws (c. 1050 BCE) the regulation of adultery had become more refined. Law 13 declares that the wife who visits a man in his own home for illicit sex will be killed along with her lover, whereas §14 declares that should their tryst occur in more neutral territory (such as an inn), the woman's husband is free to punish both parties as he sees fit. If, according to §15, the husband catches wife and lover *in flagrante delicto*, he is free to kill both of them with no further consequences. However, if it is made clear that the wife specifically seduced the lover, the man will be regarded as blameless, and the husband may impose whatever penalty upon his wife he chooses (§16).[120]

Martha Roth has noted that no such adultery clauses were present in the Neo-Babylonian laws. Instead, ten marriage contracts dating between 635 and 523 BCE contain a clause declaring that, should the wife be discovered with another man, "she will die by the iron dagger."[121] This would seem to indicate that the

---

[117] Roth 2014: 148. [118] Roth 2014: 151. [119] Roth 2014: 153.
[120] For more on these Middle Assyrian laws, see Peled 2020a: chapter 4.
[121] Roth 1988: 186–188.

death penalty was automatic in such circumstances, denying the husband any opportunity to spare his spouse.

The unequal concern with female fidelity also appears in the Bible. The basic commandments are sex-neutral (if not specifically directed at males, as masculine verbal forms are used in the Commandments): "You shall not commit adultery" (Exodus 20:13, Deuteronomy 5:17). In Leviticus 20:10 both partners die: "If a man commits adultery with the wife of his neighbor, both the adulterer and the adulteress shall be put to death."

However, the most explicit discussion of adultery appears in Numbers 5:11–31, where a wife is basically forced to drink poison if her husband even *suspects* her of adultery (excerpted):

> If a man's wife goes astray and is unfaithful to him so that another man has sexual relations with her, and this is hidden from her husband and her impurity is undetected (since there is no witness against her and she has not been caught in the act), and if feelings of jealousy come over her husband and he suspects his wife and she is impure – or if he is jealous and suspects her even though she is not impure – then he is to take his wife to the priest. The priest shall bring her and have her stand before the LORD. Then he shall take some holy water in a clay jar and put some dust from the tabernacle floor into the water. Then the priest shall put the woman under oath and say to her, "If no other man has had sexual relations with you and you have not gone astray and become impure while married to your husband, may this bitter water that brings a curse not harm you. But if you have gone astray while married to your husband and you have made yourself impure by having sexual relations with a man other than your husband" – here the priest is to put the woman under this curse – "may the LORD cause you to become a curse among your people when he makes your womb miscarry and your abdomen swell. May this water that brings a curse enter your body so that your abdomen swells or your womb miscarries." He shall make the woman drink the bitter water that brings a curse, and this water that brings a curse and causes bitter suffering will enter her. This, then, is the law of jealousy when a woman goes astray and makes herself impure while married to her husband, or when feelings of jealousy come over a man because he suspects his wife. The priest is to have her stand before the LORD and is to apply this entire law to her. The husband will be innocent of any wrongdoing, but the woman will bear the consequences of her sin.

We have far fewer data from Anatolia. Two laws from the *Hittite Laws* deal with the issue, although with a bit of ambivalence:

> §197: If a man seizes a woman in the mountains (and rapes her), the man is guilty and shall die; but if he seizes her in the house, the woman is guilty and shall die. If the woman's husband catches them (in the act) and kills them, he has committed no crime.

§198: If he brings them to the palace gate and says: "My wife shall not die," he can spare his wife's life, but he must also spare the lover ... But if he says, "Both of them shall die" ... the king may have them both killed or he may spare them.[122]

The ambivalence comes from the fact that it was not always possible to distinguish adultery from rape. The logic of §197 appears to be that the only way the male perpetrator could have gotten into the house in the first place and had sex with a woman who could have cried out for help (and thus have assistants against the assailant or at least witnesses to her lack of complicity) was that she was, in fact, complicit – thus adultery. In any other context (e.g. the mountains), rape is assumed, and the woman is deemed innocent.

Rape

This indoor/outdoor ambiguity also appears in the Bible. In Deuteronomy 22:23–27 we read:

> If a man happens to meet in a town a virgin pledged to be married and he sleeps with her, you shall take both of them to the gate of that town and stone them to death – the young woman because she was in a town and did not scream for help, and the man because he violated another man's wife. ... But if out in the country a man happens to meet a young woman pledged to be married and rapes her, only the man who has done this shall die. Do nothing to the woman; she has committed no sin deserving death. ... for the man found the young woman out in the country, and though the betrothed woman screamed, there was no one to rescue her.

Two of three biblical rape narratives – Genesis 34, Judges 19, and 2 Samuel 13 – support this same distinction. In Genesis 34: "Now Dinah, the daughter Leah had borne to Jacob, went out to visit the women of the land. When Shechem son of Hamor the Hivite, the ruler of that area, saw her, he took her and raped her." This rape takes place outside of the home, while Dinah is traveling. In Judges 19, the Levite's concubine is again raped away from home. By contrast, in 2 Samuel 13, the princess Tamar is raped by her half-brother inside of the household, in the man's actual bedroom:

> Then Amnon said to Tamar, "Bring the food here into my bedroom so I may eat from your hand." And Tamar took the bread she had prepared and brought it to her brother Amnon in his bedroom. But when she took it to him to eat, he grabbed her and said, "Come to bed with me, my sister." "No, my brother!" she said to him. "Don't force me! Such a thing should

---

[122] Bryce 2016: 314.

> not be done in Israel! Don't do this wicked thing. What about me? Where could I get rid of my disgrace? And what about you? You would be like one of the wicked fools in Israel. Please speak to the king; he will not keep me from being married to you." But he refused to listen to her, and since he was stronger than she, he raped her.

Here we have rape within the house but still recognized as rape.

Rather than seeing any of these narratives as primarily illustrations of legal ideology (the indoor/outdoor ambiguity), one should recognize that in each case the rape is a pretext for violence. In Genesis 34:25–31 Dinah's brothers use the attack on their sister as motivation to slaughter their sister's rapist and his entire community (even though they had earlier given Hamor permission to marry her). When criticized by their father for making him (and them) enemies of the people with whom they were living, the brothers simply replied, "Should our sister be treated like a whore?"

The rape and murder of the Levite's concubine likewise served as a pretext not only for waging war against the entire tribe of the Benjaminites but later, also, for the forcible taking of Benjaminite virgins whom the men of Ephraim seized as wives (Judges 21). Finally, the rape of Tamar in 2 Samuel began an intrafamilial dynamic among Tamar, her rapist brother Amnon, their brother Absalom, and their father David that eventually led to Absalom's attempt to overthrow his father (and Absalom's death). We can once again see the distinction between fiction and nonfiction mentioned in the section "Sources of Data." To whatever extent they may have been followed, the laws of Leviticus and Deuteronomy are a form of nonfiction: They indicate an ideal according to which the people were supposed to live. The tales of Dinah, Tamar, and the nameless concubine are fiction: They serve as plot devices in narratives wholly oriented around men.

In Mesopotamia, too, females' passivity was recognized in cases of rape, both for virgins and for wives. What differed over time was how the rapist was treated by the laws. Much as was the case with adultery, punishments varied throughout the codes from mandatory sentencing including the death penalty to allowing the victim's father or husband to decide the fate. Thus in the *Code of Hammurabi* it is stipulated that:

> §130: If a man pins down the wife-of-a-man who has not known a male and who resides in her father's house (i.e. a fiancée), and they seize him lying in her lap: that man will be killed, that woman will be released.[123]

---

[123] Roth 2014: 153.

By extreme contrast, the same scenario in the Middle Assyrian Laws provoked the following:

> §55: If a man forcibly seizes and rapes a maiden who is residing in her father's house, ... who is not spoken for, whose [womb(?)] is not opened, who is not taken (in marriage), and against whose father's house there is no outstanding claim – whether (the rape occurs) within the city, or in the countryside, or at night, whether in the main thoroughfare, or in a granary, or during the city festival: the father of the maiden shall take the wife of the maiden's rapist and give her over to be raped; he shall not return her to her husband, he shall take her (for himself). The father shall give his daughter, she who was the victim of the rape, to her rapist in *ahuzzatu* [marriage of a nonvirgin]. If (the rapist) has no wife: the rapist shall give "triple" the silver as the value of the maiden to her father; her rapist shall take her (in marriage); he shall not reject her. If the father does not desire this: he shall accept "triple" silver for the maiden, and he shall give his daughter (in marriage) to whomever he chooses.[124]

Even outside of the law codes the culpability of the rapist was widely recognized, and one way or another his karma was bound to catch up with him. Thus we find in the sex omens from Mesopotamia:

> If a man seizes a woman in the crossroad and has sexual relations [with her], that man will not prosper; either the hand of his god or the hand of the king will catch him.[125]

Incest

Although in modern times people make a fuss about homosexuality and its presumable condemnation in the Bible (overblown, as discussed), the *real* concern for the peoples of the ANE was incest. To no one did this apply more than the Israelites, who dedicated numerous laws in Leviticus and curses in Deuteronomy to this topic. After a general prohibition on sexually approaching any of his relatives (the laws are inevitably directed towards men) in Leviticus 18:6, the laws go into micro-details, basically divided into two general categories as observed by Ilan Peled:

> The first – and larger – group (Lev. 18:7–16) includes a man's female kin relatives with whom he was not allowed to have sexual intercourse. The second group (Lev. 17–18) includes multiple female partners with whom a man was forbidden to have contemporaneous sexual relationships. These women were not necessarily the man's relatives but were related to one another, and their proximity led to the prohibitions.[126]

---

[124] Roth 2014: 169–170.   [125] Guinan 1997: 474.   [126] Peled 2020a: 99.

These prohibitions forbade sexual intercourse with: one's mother (Leviticus 18:7), one's stepmother (Leviticus 18:8, 20:11); one's sister (Leviticus 18:9, 20:17); one's granddaughter (Leviticus 18:10); one's stepsister (Leviticus 18:11), one's aunt, either biological or through marriage (Leviticus 18:13–14; 20:19–20); one's daughter-in-law (Leviticus 18:15, 20:12); one's sister-in-law (Leviticus 18:16, 20:21); a woman and her daughter (Leviticus 18:17, 20:14); and a woman and her sister (Leviticus 18:18).[127] Punishments ranged from banishment to dying childless to death.

In case that isn't enough, there are also curses. In Deuteronomy (27:20, 22–23) we read:

> Cursed be anyone who lies with his father's wife, because he has violated his father's rights!
> Cursed be anyone who lies with his sister, either the daughter of his father or the daughter of his mother!
> Cursed be anyone who lies with his mother-in-law!

Cousins are not mentioned, but in-laws are. Basically, all members of the *bêt 'ab*, the paternal household, were included within these prohibitions, any female with whom a man might find himself sharing a house. Only one text – Deuteronomy 27:20 – indicates the logic of the law, that a son who has sex with his father's wife (presumably not his own mother?) infringes on his father's right to exclusive sexual access to the mother of his children. Otherwise, the prohibitions at least had the aim of minimizing conflict in the paternal household, keeping the *bêt 'ab* from turning into a soap opera while making a mess of inheritance rights.

The Hittite approach to incest was somewhat similar to that of the Bible, with laws regulating with what woman (singular) a man could have sex, and with what women (plural) he could have sex contemporaneously. As with the Bible, sex with direct relatives was forbidden: We already saw that §189 of the *Hittite Laws* prohibited a man from having sex with his own mother, daughter, or son. However, rather than total bans on sex with various in-laws, the *Hittite Laws* only prohibited such encounters when spouses were still alive. Thus the latter portion of §190 forbade a man from having sex with his stepmother while his father was alive but permitted it after the death of the father. Likewise, §192 allows a man to marry his sister-in-law if his wife (her sister) has died. §195a prohibits a man from sleeping with his brother's wife while the brother is alive. However, §193 actually required that a man marry his brother's widow. If the second husband dies, their father has to marry the widow. If the father dies, the father's brother has to

---

[127] There is oddly no reference to parent–child/father–daughter incest.

marry her. According to §§195b–c, a married man may not try to have sex with his wife's mother, sister, or daughter. Per §191:

> If a free man has intercourse with free sisters who have the same mother and also with their mother – one in one country and the other in another, it is not an offence. But if it happens in the same location, and he knows (the women are related), it is an unpermitted sexual pairing.[128]

In other words, if a man had sex with two sisters and their mother but didn't know that they were related because they lived in different towns, he is in nowhere nearly as much trouble as if he slept with the two sisters (and their mother) knowingly.

Unlike the biblical prohibitions that seemed aimed at maintaining peace in the household, the primary concern of the Hittite laws was to prevent sex between blood relations. However, since both divorce and travel (and infidelity) were practical realities, men (and women) were not held accountable if they accidentally had sex with a person who turned out to be a blood relative.

The Mesopotamians were less detailed in their laws. Two, possibly three, laws from the *Laws of Hammurabi* pertain to what, in modern times, would be considered incest:

> §154: If a man should know his daughter, they will banish that man from the city.
> §157: If a man, after his father('s death), should lie in the lap of his mother, they will burn them both.
> §158: If a man, after his father('s death), should be seized in the lap of his father's principal wife who had borne sons, that man will be disinherited from the father's house.[129]

In addition, §§155–156 punish the man who has sex with his daughter-in-law. Of all of these, the worst were mother–son incest (§157) and father–daughter-in-law incest (§155): Only these two led to the death penalty. A father's rape of his own daughter only led to banishment.

Bestiality

Although deities could have sex with animals (recall Ba'al and the cow), such a prerogative was not always open to humans. While the Mesopotamian corpus provides no data on the subject of bestiality,[130] the Hebrew Bible was very clear in this regard: In two out of four proscriptions the penalty was death. In the other

---

[128] Hoffner 1997: 151.   [129] Roth 2014: 155.   [130] Peled 2020a: 102; Hoffner 1973: 82.

two, the situation is identified as a perversion and the one who "lies" with an animal is cursed:

> Exodus 22:19: Whoever lies with an animal shall be put to death.
>
> Leviticus 18:23: You shall not have sexual relations with any animal and defile yourself with it, nor shall any woman give herself to an animal to have sexual relations with it: It is a perversion.
>
> Leviticus 20:15–16: If a man has sexual relations with an animal, he shall be put to death; and you shall kill the animal. If a woman approaches any animal and has sexual relations with it, you shall kill the woman and the animal; they shall be put to death, their blood is upon them.
>
> Deuteronomy 27:21: Cursed be anyone who lies with any animal.

Bestiality was simply not acceptable behavior.

The Hittites were a bit more open-minded in this regard. For the most part, their laws indicate that most forms of bestiality were illicit (ḫūrkil). Thus:

> §187: If a man has sexual relations with a cow, it is ḫūrkil; he will be put to death. They shall conduct him to the king's court. Whether the king orders him killed or spares his life, he shall not appear before the king.
>
> §188: If a man has sexual relations with a sheep, it is ḫūrkil; he will be put to death. They shall conduct him to the king's court. Whether the king orders him killed or spares his life, he shall not appear before the king.
>
> §199: If anyone has sexual relations with a pig or a dog, he shall die. They shall conduct him to the king's court. Whether the king orders him killed or spares his life, he shall not appear before the king. If an ox leaps upon a man (in sexual excitement), the ox shall die; the man shall not die. They shall substitute one sheep in the place of the man and put it to death. If a pig leaps upon a man, it is not an offence (UL ḫaratar).
>
> §200a: If a man has sexual relations with either a horse or a mule, it is not an offence, but he shall not approach the king, nor shall he become a priest.[131]

Two points stand out. First, it appears that it was acceptable to have sex with an equid, though I have yet to come across a single reasonable explanation as to why this was so.[132] However, even though it was a licit sexual union, it seems clear that the Hittites thought of it as a polluting one, insofar as the human partner was no longer permitted to approach the king – so as not to spread the impurity – and could henceforth not become a priest, presumably for the same reason.[133]

---

[131] Hoffner 2003: 118–119. See also Peled 2020b.
[132] For a history of speculations, see Peled 2020b: 148–156.   [133] Hoffner 2003: 119, n. 73.

Second, the Hittites did take note of who initiated the sexual encounter, human or animal (§199). The human was not to be held accountable if mounted by either an ox or a pig. In the case of the former, the ox was put to death. The only suggestion that such an encounter could have polluting consequences was the need to kill a sheep in the place of the human victim, thus alleviating the potential pollution. By contrast, other than shooing off the assailant, no actions need be taken in the case of attempted intercourse on the part of a pig. Again, no good explanations have been offered.

Necrophilia (Yes: Necrophilia)

Hittite Laws §190 states: "If he 'takes a position' with a dead person – a man or a woman – it is not an offence."[134]

The verb here "to take a position" is also used in a birth ritual text (KBo 17.65 obv. 5) that indicates that a husband is not supposed to "take a position" with his wife once she has hit her final trimester. So it does indeed appear that necrophilia is at issue. It is an acceptable sexual pairing (or at least not an offence).

So, to be clear: If you are a Hittite you are *not* allowed to have sex with your own mother, daughter, or son. You *may* have sex with your stepmother provided your father is dead, or your sister-in-law provided your brother is dead, and you *may* have sex with a mother and her two daughters provided the two sisters live in different cities and you did not know they were related at the time. Cows, sheep, pigs, and dogs are off-limits; horses and mules are okay with provisos; and corpses are fair game provided, presumably, they are not your mother, daughter, son, a cow, a sheep, or some combination of the above.

Conclusion

It is difficult to discuss sex in the ancient world. It is an extremely intimate act that must go through various levels of interpretation and filtering to be expressed in language and art. Many of the data pertain to deities who are not restricted by human mores or human biology – they are thus capable of marathon sex with no fear of pregnancy, and no fear of a lack of pregnancy, or worry about interpersonal dynamics, or performance anxiety. Basically, what we see is sexuality as *expressed*, not sexuality as *experienced*, and we must always remember that these are two separate things. Hopefully putting together all of the data will give at least some approximation of the reality.

In general, the residents of the ANE were what today we might term "sex positive." There was nothing innately evil about human sexuality, and it was

---

[134] Hoffner 2003: 118.

recognized as a source of joy in life. No one is ever "shackled by lust," and there is none of the scorn of the physical body and its natural processes that we see in philosophical traditions more influenced by Greek philosophy (e.g. Christianity). But heterosexuality at least had to be regulated because of the potential/need for offspring, offspring that had to fit appropriately into a structured, family-based society. Incest – however construed – also had to be regulated in order to create a more harmonious family-based society.

New, better research is desperately needed on ancient homosexuality. For too long we have been in the thrall of the Dover–Foucauldian model that did not actually pertain to the ancient world: The data only appear to be in that guise because we have specifically interpreted them in light of the Dover–Foucauldian model. Circular reasoning tends not to lead anywhere, circles being what they are. We *especially* need to stop pretending that modern attitudes and regulations of homosexuality are predicated on ancient precedent. We have criminalized (male) homosexuality based on supposed biblical precedent while blithely ignoring biblical constructions of incest (remember why Henry VIII wasn't supposed to marry Catherine of Aragon?) and purity laws regarding sex during menstruation or nocturnal emissions (which the ancients did not). Either we can be consistent or we can simply accept that the ancients are not us and figure things out for ourselves.

Perhaps most importantly, modern scholarship needs to view human sexuality as a means of positive emotional expression. Sex can be an expression of love. This rarely shows up in the scholarship. We often view sex as a power display only: Homosexuality is all about who is on top and showing dominance. Heterosexuality is not implicated as much in this respect because we already accept – thanks to patriarchy – that the man is already on top, so heterosexual dominance display is a given. Queer theory, which should have challenged this hegemonic paradigm, has been overly seduced by Foucault and thus does not provide an alternate perspective. Sex as an emotional response is never considered. Likewise, rape and adultery are thought to be comparable crimes because they threaten a man's control of his woman's body and offspring. This is true, of course, but there is more to these crimes than male property control. Even the Bible, in the tales of Dinah and Tamar, reveals how the emotional impact of rape affects society beyond the composition of the paternal household. The study of ancient sexuality is too much dominated by power dynamics and rarely, if ever, wades into the waters of emotion.

Finally, it should be underscored yet again that the ancients are not us. The ANE has become a battleground for modern sexual and gender politics, somehow on the theory that whatever they did then is germane to us now. Many gender theorists now try to show that the peoples of the ANE were gender nonbinary,¹³⁵ while biblical scholars claim that David and Jonathan were lovers.¹³⁶ And so on ... While I happen to think that both of these statements are inaccurate, that is not the point. The point is that we cannot hope to understand the ancient world if we are merely trying to find our own desires in it. It is unbelievably difficult to get into a different mind, especially when that mind is so far removed in time, space, and culture. If we merely use that mind as a vessel and fill it with our own agendas, we generate propaganda, not scholarship. In that scenario we learn *nothing* about the ancient world, the history of humanity, or any of the instructive and interesting lessons that such research might provide.

---

[135] Fassari and Frascarelli 2022, Matić 2021, Asher-Greve 2018, Helle 2018, Gaylord 2015, Nissinen 2003, McCaffrey 2002, Knapp and Meskell 1997, among many.

[136] Ackerman 2005, with further citations. Also Gilgameš and Enkidu.

References

Ackerman, Susan (2005) *When Heroes Love: The Ambiguities of Eros in the Stories of Gilgamesh and David*. Columbia University Press, New York.

Alster, Bendt (1975) *Studies in Sumerian Proverbs*. Akademisk Forlag, Copenhagen.

Asher-Greve, Julia (2018) "From La Femme to Multiple Sex/Gender." In S. Svärd and A. Garcia-Ventura (eds.) *Studying Gender in the Ancient Near East*. Eisenbrauns, University Park, PA, 15–50.

Assante, Julia. (2017) "Men Looking at Men: The Homoerotics of Power in the State Arts of Assyria." In I. Zsolnay (ed.) *Being a Man: Negotiating Ancient Constructs of Masculinity*. Routledge, London, 42–82.

— (2003) "From Whores to Hierodules: The Historiographic Invention of Mesopotamian Female Sex Professionals." In A. A. Donohue and M. D. Fullerton (eds.) *Ancient Art and Its Historiography*. Cambridge University Press, Cambridge, 13–47.

— (2002) "Sex, Magic and the Liminal Body in the Erotic Arts and Texts of the Old Babylonian Period." In S. Parpola and R. M. Whiting (eds.) *Sex and Gender in the Ancient Near East*. Neo-Assyrian Text Corpus Project, Helsinki, 27–54.

— (1998) "The KAR.KID/Ḫarimtu, Prostitute or Single Woman?" *Ugarit Forschungen* 30: 5–96.

Bachvarova, Mary R. (2017) "Wisdom of Former Days: The Manly Hittite King and Foolish Kumarbi, Father of the Gods." In I. Zsolnay (ed.) *Being a Man: Negotiating Ancient Constructs of Masculinity*. Routledge, London, 83–111.

Beckman, Gary (2016) "Birth and Motherhood among the Hittites." In S. L. Budin and J. MacIntosh Turfa (eds.) *Women in Antiquity: Real Women across the Ancient World*. Routledge, London, 319–328.

Ben-Shlomo, David and Lauren K. McCormick (2021) "Judean Pillar Figurines and 'Bed Models' from Tell en-Naṣbeh: Typology and Petrographic Analysis." *Bulletin of the American Society of Overseas Research* 382, 23–46.

Biggs, Robert D. (2002) "The Babylonian Sexual Potency Texts." In S. Parpola and R. M. Whiting (eds.) *Sex and Gender in the Ancient Near East*. Neo-Assyrian Text Corpus Project, Helsinki, 71–78.

— (1967) *ŠÀ.ZI.GA: Ancient Mesopotamian Potency Incantations*. J. J. Augustin Publisher, Locust Valley, NY.

Black, Jeremy, Graham Cunningham, Eleanor Robeson, and Gábor Zólyomi (2004) *The Literature of Ancient Sumer.* Oxford University Press, Oxford.

Bryce, Trevor (2016) "The Role and Status of Women in Hittite Society." In S. L. Budin and J. MacIntosh Turfa (eds.) *Women in Antiquity: Real Women across the Ancient World.* Routledge, London, 303–318.

(2002) *Life and Society in the Hittite World.* Oxford University Press, Oxford.

Budin, Stephanie L. (2024) "The Fads That Drive Us: From Frazer, Freud, and Foucault to Butler and Connell." In S. L. Budin and C. J. Tully (eds.) *A Century of James Frazer's* The Golden Bough: *Shaking the Tree, Breaking the Bough.* Routledge, New York, 117–136.

(2023) *Gender in the Ancient Near East.* Routledge, New York.

(2021) *Freewomen, Patriarchal Authority, and the Accusation of Prostitution.* Routledge, New York.

(2019) "Phallic Fertility in Egypt and the Ancient Near East." In N. Hopwood, R. Flemming, and L. Kassell (eds.) *Reproduction from Antiquity to the Present.* Cambridge University Press, Cambridge, 25–38.

(2015) "Fertility and Gender in the Ancient Near East." In M. Masterson, N. Sorkin Rabinowitz, and J. Robeson (eds.) *Sex in Antiquity: Exploring Gender and Sexuality in the Ancient World.* Routledge, London, 30–49.

Chavalas, Mark W. (ed.) (2014) *Women in the Ancient Near East.* Routledge Sourcebooks for the Ancient World. Routledge, London.

Cooper, Jerrold S. (1997) "Gendered Sexuality in Sumerian Love Poetry." In I. L. Finkel and M. J. Geller (eds.) *Sumerian Gods and Their Representations.* Styx Publications, Groningen, 85–97.

(1980) "*Enlil und Ninlil: Ein sumerischer Mythos aus Nippur* by Hermann Behrens (Review Article)." *Journal of Cuneiform Studies* 32:3, 175–188.

Dalley, Stephanie (2001) Review of R. Mattila's *The King's Magnates* (SAAS XI), published in *Bibliotheca Orientalis* LVIII:1–2, 197–206.

(1989) *Myths from Mesopotamia.* Oxford University Press, Oxford.

Dover, Kenneth J. (1978/1989) *Greek Homosexuality.* Harvard University Press, Cambridge, MA.

Dowson, Thomas A. (2008) "Queering Sex and Gender in ancient Egypt." In C. Graves-Brown (ed.) *Sex and Gender in Ancient Egypt: "Don your wig for a joyful hour."* The Classical Press of Wales, Swansea, 27–46.

Fassari, Letteria Grazia and Raffaella Frascarelli (2022) "Embodying the Past: The Case of the Goddess on Lion at Hasanlu." In K. De Graef, A. Garcia-Ventura, A. Goddeeris, and B. Alpert Nakhai (eds.) *The Mummy under the Bed: Essays on Gender and Methodology in the Ancient Near East.* Zaphon, Münster, 253–287.

Foster, Benjamin R. (1993) *Before the Muses: An Anthology of Akkadian Literature*. CDL Press, Bethesda, MD.

Foucault, Michel. (1985/1990) *The Use of Pleasure*. Vintage Books, New York.

Gaylord, Kristen (2015) "A Royal Queer: Hatshepsut and Gender Construction in Ancient Egypt." *Shift* 8, 49–59.

George, Andrew R. (1999) *The Epic of Gilgamesh: The Babylonian Epic Poem and Other Texts in Akkadian and Sumerian*. Penguin Books, London.

Glassner, Jean-Jacques (1992) "Inanna et les Me." In M. de Jong Ellis (ed.) *Nippur at the Centennial*. Occasional Publications of the Samuel Noah Kramer Fund, 14. Philadelphia, PA, 55–86.

Guinan, Ann K. (2022) "The Female Gaze: The Subjected Body in Tablet 103 of *Šumma alū* Omens 1–7." In K. De Graef, A. Garcia-Ventura, A. Goddeeris, and B. Alpert Nakhai (eds.) *The Mummy under the Bed: Essays on Gender and Methodology in the Ancient Near East*. Zaphon, Münster, 57–87.

(2002) "Erotomancy: Scripting the Erotic." In S. Parpola and R. M. Whiting (eds.) *Sex and Gender in the Ancient Near East*. Neo-Assyrian Text Corpus Project, Helsinki, 185–202.

(1997) "Auguries of Hegemony: The Sex Omens of Mesopotamia." In M. Wyke (ed.) *Gender and the Body in the Ancient Mediterranean*. Blackwell Publishers, Oxford, 38–55. (Reprint of 1996 publication in *Gender & History* 9:3, 462–479).

Guinan, Ann K. and Peter Morris (2017) "Mesopotamia before and after Sodom: Colleagues, Crack Troops, Comrades-in-Arms." In I. Zsolnay (ed.) *Being a Man: Negotiating Ancient Constructs of Masculinity*. Routledge, London, 150–175.

Helle, Sophus (2018) "'Only in Dress?' Methodological Concerns Regarding Non-Binary Gender." In S. L. Budin, M. Cifarelli, A. Garcia-Ventura, and A. Millet Albà (eds.) *Gender and methodology in the ancient Near East*. Proceedings of the Second Workshop Held in Barcelona, February 1–3, 2017. Barcelona, Edicions de la Universitat de Barcelona, 41–53.

Hess, Richard S. (2003) "Contracts: Alalakh." In W. W. Hallo and K. L. Younger (eds.) *The Context of Scripture*, Vol. 3. Brill, Leiden, 249–254.

Hoffner, Harry A. Jr. (2003) "Hittite Laws." In W. W. Hallo and K. L. Younger (eds.) *The Context of Scripture*, Vol. 2. Brill, Leiden, 106–119.

(1998) *Hittite Myths*. 2nd ed. Scholars Press, Atlanta, GA.

(1997) *The Laws of the Hittites: A Critical Edition*. Brill, Leiden.

(1987) "Paskuwatti's Ritual against Sexual Impotence (CTH 406)." *Aula Orientalis* 5, 271–287.

(1973) "Incest, Sodomy and Bestiality in the Ancient Near East." In H. A. Hoffner (ed.) *Orient and Occident: Essays Presented to Cyrus*

H. Gordon on the Occasion of His Sixty-Fifth Birthday. Neukirchener Verlag, Neukirchen-Vluyn, 81–90.

Jacobsen, Thorkild (1987) *The Harps That Once . . . : Sumerian Poetry in Translation*. Yale University Press, New Haven, CT.

Jones, Philip (2003) "Embracing Inana: Legitimation and Mediation in the Ancient Mesopotamian Sacred Marriage Hymn Iddin-Dagan A." *Journal of the American Oriental Society* 123:2, 291–302.

Justel, Josué J. (2016) "Women, Gender and Law at the Dawn of History." In S. L. Budin and J. MacIntosh Turfa (eds.) *Women in Antiquity: Real Women Across the Ancient World*. Routledge, London, 77–100.

(2014) *Mujeres y derecho en el Próximo Oriente Antiguo: La presencia de mujeres en los textos jurídocos cuneiformes del segundo y primer milenios a.C.* Libros Pórtico, Zaragoza.

Knapp, A. Bernard and Lynn Meskell (1997) "Bodies of Evidence on Prehistoric Cyprus." *Cambridge Archaeological Journal* 7:2, 183–204.

Kramer, Samuel N. (1985) "BM 23631: Bread for Enlil, Sex for Inanna." *Orientalia*, Nova Series 54, no. 1/2, 117–132.

Leick, Gwendolyn (1994) *Sex and Eroticism in Mesopotamian Literature*. Routledge, London.

Levine, Baruch (2002) "'Seed' versus 'Womb': Expressions of Male Dominance in Biblical Israel." In S. Parpola and R. M. Whiting (eds.) *Sex and Gender in the Ancient Near East*. Neo-Assyrian Text Corpus Project, Helsinki, 337–344.

Lewis, Theodore J. (1997) "The Birth of the Grecious Gods." In S. Parker (ed.) *Ugaritic Narrative Poetry*. Scholars Press, Atlanta, GA, 205–214.

Matić, Uroš (2021) *Violence and Gender in Ancient Egypt*. Routledge, London.

McCaffrey, Kathleen (2002) "Reconsidering Gender Ambiguity in Mesopotamia: Is a Beard Just a Beard?" In S. Parpola and R. M. Whiting (eds.) *Sex and Gender in the Ancient Near East*. Neo-Assyrian Text Corpus Project, Helsinki, 379–392.

McCormick, Lauren. (2023) "Paint: A Fourth Dimension of Sculpture." *Expedition* 64:3, 92–93.

Michałowski, Piotr (1996) "Ancient Poetics." In M. E. Vogelzang and H. L. J. Vanstiphout (eds.) *Mesopotamian Poetic Language: Sumerian and Akkadian*. Styx, Groningen, 141–153.

Miller, J. L. (2010) "Paskuwatti's Ritual: Remedy for Impotence or Antidote to Homosexuality?" *Journal of Ancient Near Eastern Religions* 10:1, 83–89.

Nissinen, Martti. (2003) *Prophet and Prophecy in the Ancient Near East*. Society of Biblical Literature, Atlanta, GA.

(1998) *Homoeroticism in the Biblical World: A Historical Perspective.* Fortress Press, Minneapolis, MN.

Olyan, Saul M. (1994) "'And with a Male You Shall Not Lie the Lying down of a Woman': On the Meaning and Significance of Leviticus 18:22 and 20:13." *Journal of the History of Sexuality* 5:2, 179–206.

Paglia, Camille (1991) "Junk Bonds and Corporate Raiders: Academe in the Hour of the Wolf" Reviewed Work(s): *One Hundred Years of Homosexuality: And Other Essays on Greek Love* by David M. Halperin: *The Constraints of Desire: The Anthropology of Sex and Gender in Ancient Greec*e by John J. Winkler" *Arion* 1:2, 139–212.

Pardee, Dennis (2002) *Ritual and Cult at Ugarit.* Society of Biblical Literature, Atlanta, GA.

Parker, Simon (ed.) (1997) *Ugaritic Narrative Poetry.* Scholars Press, Atlanta, GA.

Parpola, Simo and Kazuko Watanabe (1988) *Neo-Assyrian Treaties and Loyalty Oaths.* State Archives of Assyria 2. Neo-Assyrian Text Corpus Project. Helsinki.

Parpola, Simo and Robert M. Whiting (eds.) (2002) *Sex and Gender in the Ancient Near East.* University of Helsinki, Helsinki .

Paul, Shalom M. (2002) "The Shared Legacy of Sexual Metaphors and Euphemisms in Mesopotamian and Biblical Literature." In S. Parpola and R. M. Whiting (eds.) *Sex and Gender in the Ancient Near East.* Neo-Assyrian Text Corpus Project, Helsinki, 489–498.

Peled, Ilan (2020a) *Law and Gender in the Ancient Near East and the Hebrew Bible.* Routledge, New York.

(2020b) "Bestiality in Hittite Thought." *JANES* 34, 136–177.

(2016) *Masculinities and Third Gender: The Origins and Nature of an Institutionalized Gender Otherness in the Ancient Near East.* Ugarit-Verlag, Münster.

Roth, Martha T. (2014) "Women and Law." In M. W. Chavalas (ed.) *Women in the Ancient Near East: A Sourcebook.* Routledge, London, 144–174.

(2006) "Marriage, Divorce, and the Prostitute in Ancient Mesopotamia." In C. A. Faraone and L. K. McClure (eds.) *Prostitutes and Courtesans in the Ancient World.* University of Wisconsin Press, Madison, WI, 21–39.

(1988) "'She Will Die by the Iron Dagger': Adultery and Neo-Babylonian Marriage." *JESHO* 31, 186–206.

Satlow, Michael L. (2014) *How the Bible Became Holy.* Yale University Press, New Haven, CT.

Scurlock, JoAnn (2014) "Medicine and Healing Magic." In M. Chavalas (ed.) *Women in the Ancient Near East*. Routledge Sourcebooks for the Ancient World. Routledge, London, 101–143.

Suter, Claudia E. (2000) *Gudea's Temple Building: The Representation of an Early Mesopotamian Ruler in Text and Image*. Cuneiform Monographs 17. Styx Publications, Groningen.

Von Soden, Wolfram and Joachim Oelsner (1991) "Ein spät-altbabylonisches *pārum*-Preislied für Ištar." *Orientalia*, Nova Series 60, no. 4, 339–343.

Wegner, Ilse (1981) *Gestalt und Kult der Ištar-Šawuška in Kleinasien*. Verlag Butzon & Bercker Kevelaer, Neukirchen-Vluyn.

Whittaker, G. (2002) "Linguistic Anthropology and the Study of Emesal as (a) Women's Language." In S. Parpola and R. M. Whiting (eds.) *Sex and Gender in the Ancient Near East*. Neo-Assyrian Text Corpus Project, Helsinki, 633–644.

Wiggermann, Frans A. M. (2010) "Sexualität (sexuality), A: Mesopotamia." *Reallexikon der Assyriologie*, 12, 410–426.

Zisa, Gioele (2021) *The Loss of Male Sexual Desire in Ancient Mesopotamia*. De Gruyter, Berlin.

Zsolnay, Ilona (2017) *Being a Man: Negotiating Ancient Constructs of Masculinity*. Routledge, New York.

(2014) "Gender and Sexuality: Ancient Near East." In J. M. O'Brien (ed.) *The Oxford Encyclopedia of the Bible and Gender Studies*, Vol. 1. Oxford University Press, Oxford, 273–287.

Cambridge Elements

The Ancient Near Eastern World and the Bible

Christopher B. Hays
*Fuller Theological Seminary and
University of Pretoria, South Africa*

Christopher B. Hays is D. Wilson Moore Professor of Old Testament and Ancient Near Eastern Studies at Fuller Theological Seminary, and a Research Associate of the University of Pretoria, South Africa. He has served as the U.S. State Department Educational and Cultural Affairs Annual Professor at the Albright Institute of Archaeological Research in Jerusalem, and as President of the Pacific Coast Region of Society of Biblical Literature. Hays is the author of *Hidden Riches: A Textbook for the Comparative Study of the Old Testament and the Ancient Near East* (2014), *Death in the Iron Age II and in First Isaiah* (2011), and *Wenamun's Prophetic Mission: Theocratic Rhetoric in Egypt and the Hebrew Bible* (2025). He holds a PhD in Hebrew Bible from Emory University, and an MA in Egyptology from UCLA, and an MDiv from Princeton Theological Seminary. hays@fuller.edu

Brent A. Strawn
Duke University

Brent A. Strawn is D. Moody Smith Distinguished Professor of Old Testament and Professor of Law at Duke University and McDonald Distinguished Fellow in Law and Religion at Emory University's Center for the Study of Law and Religion. He has edited over thirty volumes to date, including the award-winning volumes *The Oxford Encyclopedia of the Bible and Law* (2015) and *The World Around the Old Testament: The People and Places of the Ancient Near East* (2016). He has authored over 300 articles, essays, and contributions to reference works, as well as seven books, most recently *Unwavering Holiness: Pivotal Moments in the Book of Isaiah* (2025, with Walter Brueggemann). He sits on several editorial boards and served as translator and editor for both the Common English Bible (2011) and the New Revised Standard Version updated edition (2022). In 2023, Strawn was awarded a grant from the National Endowment for the Humanities. bstrawn@div.duke.edu

About the series

The Ancient Near Eastern World and the Bible Elements series explores the field of ancient Near Eastern studies and its developments in an approachable, holistic, and integrated way, focusing on intersections with the Bible and biblical studies. The ancient Near East (ANE) encompasses a vast temporal and geographical terrain, including the peoples and cultures, history and religion that gave rise to and shaped the biblical texts. The ANEWB series explores these areas, providing thorough overviews and introductions to a host of ANE topics, organized into four major streams that include "Peoples and Empire," "Social History," "Religion," and "Texts," with the primary focus on those materials that are of greatest significance to understanding ancient Israel and the biblical world. In the series, scholars make the latest and best scholarship available in highly accessible ways, introducing readers to the essentials of the topic in question while also conveying distinctive viewpoints and capturing new developments.

Cambridge Elements

The Ancient Near Eastern World and the Bible

Elements in the Series

Sex and Sexuality in the Ancient Near East
Stephanie Lynn Budin

A full series listing is available at: www.cambridge.org/ENEB

For EU product safety concerns, contact us at Calle de José Abascal, 56–1°, 28003 Madrid, Spain or eugpsr@cambridge.org.

www.ingramcontent.com/pod-product-compliance
Lightning Source LLC
LaVergne TN
LVHW011857060526
838200LV00054B/4383